BACK

TO THE

ALTAR

A Call to Spiritual Awakening

Thomas E.   *David A.*

TRASK WOMACK

GPH

Springfield, Missouri

02-0328

To all those who yearn for a fresh
outpouring of the Holy Spirit
for the twenty-first century

3rd Printing 1995

Library of Congress Catalog Card Number 94-076336
International Standard Book Number 0-88243-328-8

Printed in the United States of America

Table of Contents

Table of Contents

Preface

This call to spiritual awakening was but a few months in the writing, but its preparation came from the decades of experience of two sons of Assemblies of God preachers. A great number of people, from leaders to laymen, have contributed greatly to the writing of this book, for none who ever have known the wonders of Pentecostal fire can ever be satisfied with embers of a waning revival.

Our purpose is not to call for a return to the early twentieth century but to point our Fellowship to the same powerful source from which sprang the revival of our forefathers—the original Christianity of the New Testament church. In the following paragraphs we each will speak separately, but in the rest of the book we will generally speak as one.

Thomas E. Trask:

This co-authored book is a result of the awareness God has placed within our hearts of the work of the Holy Spirit. The subject can be summed up in two words: *desire* and *need*.

The first work of the Holy Spirit in the life of the believer and thus in the church of Jesus Christ is to cause us to sense our need of God. With the systems of the world failing to supply answers to human needs, it is imperative that the church arise to be the hospital to save lives, to bring healing to those who are sick, and to comfort those who are hurting. Revival will bring spiritual life and sensitivity to the church. It will then seize the opportunities God gives to it for ministry. Eye scales will drop off, and believers will see as Christ sees and feel as He feels. We will then do His bidding.

It is also the work of the Holy Spirit to place a desire, a hunger, in our hearts for more of God. As we look at the needs of the world and our inability to meet those needs, we will sense our complete dependence upon the Lord. This will cause us to run to Him with a burning desire for the enabling power of the Holy Spirit. This desire will give us a hunger for His presence, a thirst for His Word, and a burden that can be satisfied only through prayer. The Scripture states that when "Zion travailed, she brought forth . . ." (Isaiah 66:8). We believe God is creating something, born of the Spirit, within the hearts of our Assemblies of God ministers and laymen that will produce a heaven-sent, Holy Ghost revival.

David A. Womack:

A few years ago, I went back to the mountain-goat farm where I spent some of my early childhood. Everything had changed. The goats were gone, of course, but so were the two-room house, the barn, the pig pens, and the hay. Another house had been built, but it had burnt to the ground, leaving only the stone foundation. Beavers had dammed up the creek where I used to fish and turned it into a pond. Worst of all, grass had grown over all my old paths. Nearly half a century of summer growth and winter snows had erased all signs that I had ever been there.

We face a similar problem in the Assemblies of God. The old paths are gone, and we have few people left who remember where those paths once began or where they used to lead. With the passing of generations, we can no longer depend upon our memories of the early Pentecostal movement but must experience a new spiritual awakening for the twenty-first century.

The purpose of this book is not to find fault but to seek solutions. Revival is survival—not a return to anything we have been before but an awakening of original, New Testament, apostolic Christianity, born on the Day of Pentecost. That is the whole subject of this book.

Let the reader make no attempt to comprehend how I came to

work with Thomas Trask on this book. There is an old saying among the Mossi tribesmen of Burkina Faso, West Africa: "The stone that got mixed in with the beans got into the pot." I rejoice to find myself under the leadership of godly Pentecostal men whom God has called to lead this revival, General Superintendent Thomas E. Trask, Assistant General Superintendent Charles T. Crabtree, General Secretary George O. Wood, and General Treasurer James K. Bridges.

Throughout the book I will identify when the words are specifically those of Thomas Trask. However, the reader must recognize that the entire book has grown out of a cooperative effort, with many fervent conversations and times of a great sense of divine anointing. These may be our words, but we both believe that we have worked under a mandate from God.

In addition to our material, the book includes contributions from executive officers and others, which the authors wrote specifically for this project. These are identified by author as they occur.

All Bible references in this book are from the King James Version unless otherwise identified.

We have made no attempt to offer a comprehensive treatment of the subject of revival. In fact, both of us feel that the words *spiritual awakening* come closest to the need we sense for the Pentecostal movement. Thoughtful readers will suggest other Bible passages we could have used or offer other advice about what ought to be done. Indeed, we intend that this book will set off a whole new wave of intense innovation, anointed preaching, and inspired writing across our Movement to bring America back to its knees before God.

1

Awake, Thou That Sleepest!

From childhood we have heard that old line—"What this church needs is not a revival but a resurrection!"

The truth is that it makes little difference how we identify the condition of the church. For a people commissioned to spread the gospel to every man, woman, and child on the face of the earth, whether the church is sick, asleep, or dead is of little consequence; the divine task is not getting done. If the church is sick, we have a Healer infinitely capable of blessing us with new life. If it is sleeping on the job, we need a wake-up call. If it is dead, we must remind ourselves of Ezekiel's vision of the valley of dry bones.

Dry Bones (Ezekiel 37:1–14)

A typical characteristic of Pentecostal preaching is that we use a Bible story to make applications to our present lives. It is not an allegorical approach to Scripture, for we strongly believe that the Bible stories are true; it is rather that we see personal meaning in the stories beyond their historical value.

During the Babylonian captivity in the sixth century B.C., the Spirit of the Lord carried the prophet Ezekiel to a valley full of dry bones and asked, "Can these bones live?"

Ezekiel, who learned the bones represented the spiritual condition of the people of God, saw no cause for encouragement but replied, "O Lord God, thou knowest."

Ezekiel's task might have been to gather up the bones and give them a decent burial, but God had a different plan. Because He never gives up on His people, God said, "Prophesy upon these bones, and say unto them, O ye dry bones, hear the word of the Lord." There were no programs, no memorial services, no theme music playing in the background. God said, "Preach!" The answer to the problem of dryness was to preach with such power that the very dead would be raised.

God declared, "I will cause breath to enter into you, and ye shall live . . . and ye shall know that I am the Lord."

Ezekiel wrote, "So I prophesied as I was commanded: and as I prophesied, there was a noise, and behold a shaking, and the bones came together, bone to . . . bone." Sinews and flesh came upon them, and skin covered them.

Then God said, "Prophesy unto the wind . . . and say, Thus saith the Lord God. . . ."

Ezekiel knew that wind was associated with the Spirit of God. The Hebrew word for spirit was *rûach,* which also meant "breath" or "wind." Ezekiel stood before the congregation of dry bones and prophesied to the wind, and "the breath came into them, and they lived, and stood up upon their feet, an exceeding great army."

Today, neither the need nor the solution has changed. God's cure for a dead church still is preaching. No, more than that—it is prophesying! Ezekiel did not deliver a three-point sermon on his theology of dying; he heard from God and delivered the Word of the Lord. He spoke with the authority of firsthand experience with God and declared, "Thus saith the Lord God. . . ." There had been no great move among the lifeless bones, no organization, no crying out for help. The Spirit of the Lord carried Ezekiel to that valley and gave him a mandate to believe in the impossible, to dare to proclaim God's Word to a disjointed and unhearing people, and to see that dead congregation rise again to new life.

Let us make one more observation. God said, "Prophesy," and Ezekiel did. Unrealistic and futile as it seemed, he stepped forth in the knowledge of his new experience with God and obeyed Him in the face of every natural evidence that those people were dead.

Once Ezekiel had done his part, God did His part. It was not Ezekiel's responsibility to perform the miracle but to preach

God's Word to the ultimate indifferent crowd. Then, and only then, did God do His miracle on those dry bones. Ezekiel responded to God, and God further responded to Ezekiel's obedience. Next, Ezekiel prophesied to the wind. We can just see him with his cloak flying and his arms outstretched to the sky, as he cried out again, "Thus saith the Lord God. . . ." It was then that God gave new life to that dead congregation.

So, which do we need today, revival or resurrection? It makes no difference. Our God can heal the sick, deliver the depressed, or raise the dead with equal application of His mighty power. We hear it said that we need an awakening, a restoration, a revitalization, a renewal, or a rejuvenation. These are only words; what we need is what Ezekiel had—the inspiration of a fresh encounter with the Spirit of God.

It does no good to sit around bemoaning our scattered and desiccated condition. What we need is a revival of prophetic preaching that dares to say, "Thus saith the Lord God. . . ."

You would think that the church would be unusually aroused at such a time as this. At the end of a powerful century of Pentecostal revival, we are about to begin a new millennium. Prophecies of the soon return of our Lord abound, and even the secular world feels that something is about to happen. A movement that began in one room in Topeka, Kansas, in 1901 now numbers its believers in the millions in more than 130 nations. And yet, just when we needed to launch our final drive we began to hesitate and stumble over our own feet.

Let's look at the core of the problem. Early in the twentieth century the Pentecostal movement was born in a great explosion of spiritual power as the church rediscovered the baptism in the Holy Spirit and original, New Testament, apostolic, Pentecostal Christianity. The newness of that experience now has worn off, and we are trying to wage our spiritual warfare in the armor of a different generation. With each passing year, the spiritual intensity of the original revival is diluted, and we become increasingly like the very churches from which our people once fled or were dismissed.

Is everything wrong? Certainly not! We are a great church with a promising future. In many ways we have grown and matured. We rank highly in nearly every category by which churches measure themselves. We are popular, professional, and poised. Yet, when we lift up our eyes and measure our success by the ungathered grain still standing in the fields instead of what we have stored in our barns, we fall embarrassingly short. Just when we had gotten big enough to have any chance of carrying out the Great Commission, we began to lose our momentum and close our heavy eyes in slumber.

One dictionary defines *sleep* as "a natural, regularly occurring condition of rest for the body and mind, during which there is little or no conscious thought or movement." Yes, perhaps that is our condition.

Jairus' Daughter (Luke 8:26 to 9:2)

There is another Bible story that aptly illustrates our plight and its only solution. Jesus had just confronted a demon-possessed man "of the country of the Gadarenes" and had cast the devils into a herd of pigs (Luke 8:26–40). The Jewish farmers, forbidden to eat pork, were compromising their faith by raising pigs to feed the Roman garrison stationed on the eastern ridge above the Sea of Galilee. No one dared complain when the pigs ran headlong into the sea and were drowned.

Jesus told the man, "Return to thine own house, and show how great things God hath done unto thee." Yet, the people were so afraid of spiritual phenomena that they begged Jesus to leave them and not to do any more signs and wonders in their midst—a mysterious reaction of religious people who for some unexplained reason prefer worship without wonders, sermons without spirit, and prayer without response. Except for social reasons, why would anyone attend a church where nothing supernatural ever happens, where prayers are never answered, and where shouts of praise are never heard as people are healed or delivered?

Following that event, Jesus was returning along the road to Capernaum when Jairus, the chief rabbi, or ruler, of the synagogue, came out to meet Him. The religious leader fell at Jesus' feet "and besought him that he would come into his house: for he had one only daughter, about twelve years of age, and she lay a dying."

As they passed through a throng of people on their way to the rabbi's house, a woman with an affliction of twelve years reached out and touched Him and was instantly healed. Jesus said, "Somebody hath touched me: for I perceive that virtue is gone out of me." Many of our pastors, missionaries, and evangelists have testified of the physical weakness they feel after a healing service. The laying on of hands is obviously much more than a ritual or act of obedience; there is a transfer of power when people are healed.

As Jesus was telling the healed woman, "Thy faith hath made thee whole," someone from the rabbi's house came and reported, "Thy daughter is dead." That was the human evaluation of her condition—dead, finished, hopeless!

Luke wrote, "But . . . ." (Oh, how important is that little word as faith contradicts facts!) He wrote, "But when Jesus heard it, he answered him, saying, Fear not: believe only, and she shall be made whole"—put away fear, have faith, and find fulfillment of the promises of God.

When Jesus came to the house, the flute players and a wailing crowd had already started her funeral (Matthew 9:23). There was no doubt in anyone's mind that the girl was dead. Jesus allowed only Peter, James, John, and the parents to go into the room where the dead girl lay. Everyone was weeping, but Jesus said, "Weep not; she is not dead, but sleepeth" (Luke 8:52). The mourners laughed Him to scorn, knowing that she was dead; but He put them all out, took the girl by the hand, and called to her in Aramaic, "Talitha cumi!" (Maid, arise!) "Her spirit came again," and Jesus told the family to get her something to eat.

The story really happened and is recorded in three of the Gospels (Matthew 9:18–26; Mark 5:22–43; Luke 8:41–56). At the same time, the story contains principles that may be applied to many areas of life, not the least of which is the church.

At first, Jesus was surrounded by a curious but largely uncommitted crowd not too different from people today who are attracted to popular religion. Jesus narrowed the group down to His twelve disciples and the immediate family, then further confined the participating minority to Peter, James, and John (His inner circle) and the parents.

Whether the girl needed a revival or a resurrection made no difference to Jesus. His problem was not with the dead girl but with the unbelieving people who fatalistically accepted death as final and scorned any suggestion to the contrary. He had to put the doubters out of the room before He could work the miracle of her awakening. Luke wrote, "Her spirit came again, and she arose straightway" (Luke 8:55). Might it be that the Lord will have to have some of us out of the room before He can do miracles and revive His church? Like Jairus' daughter, we need our spirit back again!

It is no coincidence that immediately after this event Jesus "called his twelve disciples together, and gave them power and authority over all devils, and to cure diseases. And he sent them to preach the kingdom of God, and to heal the sick" (Luke 6:1). This is still the task of the church! How, then, can we dare to be conservative Christians in the face of the example of Jesus' ministry and His instructions to His disciples? The world will not be won by quiet Christians with folded hands; world evangelization will require fiery-eyed witnesses of the presence and power of Jesus Christ to save, to heal, and to deliver.

The story of our church at the end of the second millennium after the coming of Christ could not be illustrated better than in the raising of Jairus' daughter. The church is dead, and everybody knows it. The parents (the previous generation) cannot help. Church leaders cannot do it alone and in fact are often elected by conservative congregations to keep the church from getting out of hand. Even the inner circle of those closest to the Lord cannot cause revival to happen. The truth is that only Jesus can awaken this dead or dying church and restore it to its full life. Only then will the church go forth in renewed power (dynamic force) and authority (permission to use that force) to proclaim the gospel, control evil, and bring healing to our land.

Those two stories—Ezekiel's Valley of Dry Bones and Jairus' Daughter—are what this book is all about. Revival does not start with the multitude, the church, or even any inner circle of those closest to Christ. Rather it begins when somebody calls out to Jesus for help and asks Him into the house. Then, Jesus—and He alone—can do the miracle that will awaken the church to newness of life!

The question is: Does Jesus want us to be revived? The determining factor in the Jairus story was not a sovereign decision made in heaven but a divine response to the cry of a believing father. Jesus responds to our cries for help . . . and if we ever needed help in raising the dead we need it today!

The story started with Jairus requesting Jesus to heal his daughter. Every revival begins with prayer, often with fasting. In his first week in office, General Superintendent Thomas

Trask wrote to Assemblies of God evangelists, "Call the church to prayer and fasting. It is going to be prayer that will open the door through which revival will come."

Did Anybody Set the Alarm Clock? (Ephesians 5)

After calling on Christians to "be . . . followers of God, as dear children" (Ephesians 5:1) and exhorting them to love and personal holiness, Paul wrote, "Wherefore he saith, Awake thou that sleepest, and arise from the dead, and Christ shall give thee light" (5:14).* What we need, then, is to awaken from our spiritual sleep and arise from the dead! Again, it makes no difference how severe our condition. Spiritually asleep or dead, we must awake, arise, and advance in the light.

Look at what the Bible says about waking up from our spiritual sleep:

Judges 5:12 says, "Awake, awake, Deborah: awake, awake, utter a song: arise, Barak, and lead thy captivity captive." It was time for Israel to arise and go to battle, but they had to wake up the leaders first.

Look at Psalm 17:15—"As for me, I will behold thy face in righteousness: I shall be satisfied, when I awake, with thy likeness." Our goal is to be like Jesus.

For those who trust in buildings and public image, in Habakkuk 2:19 the prophet cried out, "Woe unto him that saith to the wood, Awake; to the dumb stone, Arise, it shall teach! Behold, it is laid over with gold and silver, and there is no breath [spirit] at all in the midst of it." There in a nutshell are the remains of a materialistic church in desperate need of a spiritual revival.

Paul wrote in Romans 13:11, "And that, knowing the time, that now it is high time to awake out of sleep: for now is our salvation nearer than when we believed." If early Pentecostals expected the soon coming of Jesus Christ in their day, we must be much closer to that blessed event now!

Listen to 1 Corinthians 15:34—"Awake to righteousness, and

---

*It is uncertain what Paul was quoting in this passage. The verse probably should be translated "This is why it is said . . .," as in the NIV. Some scholars believe it to be a quote from an Early Church hymn.

sin not; for some have not the knowledge of God: I speak this to your shame." Yes, it is a shame how worldly the church has become, how far from God and how close to the world.

In Ephesians 5, where Paul said, "Awake thou that sleepest, and arise from the dead, and Christ shall give thee light," he also called on Christians to "be . . . followers of God" and to "walk in love." He went on to say, "But fornication, and all uncleanness, or covetousness, let it not be once named among you, as becometh saints; neither filthiness, nor foolish talking, nor jesting, which are not convenient: but rather giving of thanks." Such sins as sexual immorality, unclean life-styles, greed, or idolatry do not have "any inheritance in the kingdom of Christ and of God." Of people who commit such sins, Paul says to the church, "Be not ye therefore partakers with them."

The church must be righteous, holy, set apart from the world for the glory of God. Paul went on to say, "And be not drunk with wine, wherein is excess; but be filled with the Spirit" (Ephesians 5:18). Paul obviously was comparing the response of Christians upon being filled with the Spirit to that of people who have drunk excessively of wine! We recall the crowd's impression of the sights and sounds of people being filled with the Spirit on the Day of Pentecost, that the 120 were drunk on wine (Acts 2:15). These passages give us an indication of what God expects in our services. Indeed, the very next passage in Ephesians describes a church service—"Speaking to yourselves in psalms and hymns and spiritual songs, singing and making melody in your heart to the Lord; giving thanks always for all things unto God and the Father in the name of our Lord Jesus Christ" (Ephesians 5:19–20).

Paul went on in the rest of Ephesians 5 to compare the relationship of Christ and His church to that of a husband and wife. Certainly that relationship is supposed to be one of emotion, love, passion. Paul said in this same passage, "This is a great mystery: but I speak concerning Christ and the church." There is no indication in Scripture that the Lord ever intended that the church should be quietly conservative. On the contrary, in His church He expects the full range of human emotion, expressed with great passion for Him and compassion on people. Try as we might to identify our churches with certain elements of society or with historical traditions, there is no place in a Pentecostal church for nonbiblical religion or practices.

Sleeping through the Glory (Luke 9:28–36)

One of the most disturbing verses in the Bible is Luke 9:32—"But Peter and they that were with him were heavy with sleep: and when they were awake, they saw his glory."

Picture this incredible scene: Jesus had taken His inner-circle disciples—the ones closest to Him—up to the top of the Mount of Transfiguration. As Jesus prayed, "the fashion of his countenance was altered, and his raiment was white and glistering. And, behold, there talked with him two men, which were Moses and Elijah: who appeared in glory."

And what were the future Christian leaders doing? *They were asleep* at the very time that the Lord was revealing himself in His glory!

Is this not our condition today? How could a movement that once was the fastest-growing church in the world find itself in the awful condition that in one twelve-month period it took an average of four churches to add one new person to our Fellowship's Sunday morning church attendance?

The key to revival is prayer. When they came down from the Mount of Transfiguration, Jesus and His disciples were faced with the challenge of a demon-possessed boy. Jesus said, "This kind goeth not out but by prayer and fasting" (Matthew 17:21). The glory on the mountaintop was wonderful, but they still needed to fast and pray to overcome evil.

Charles G. Finney said, "Prayer is an essential link in the chain of causes that lead to a revival."

So let's wake up, rub the sleep from our eyes, look upon His glory, and go once more into serious prayer and fasting. We need a new spiritual awakening in the Assemblies of God!

2

A Call to Revival

I first spoke of this book to Thomas Trask in the foyer of Central Assembly of God in Springfield, Missouri. He had just been elected general superintendent at the Minneapolis General Council in August 1993, and I had just returned to Springfield after an absence of fifteen years to work with Gospel Publishing House under General Manager Joseph W. Kilpatrick. In early September we had had a Sunday morning service with such a profound sense of the presence of God that Pastor Philip Wannenmacher did not get to preach as the congregation continued in praise and manifestations of the gifts of the Spirit. In those days we knew that this book was ordered of the Lord.

I interviewed Thomas Trask soon after he moved into his new office in December 1993. In the following two chapters I present to you the call to revival of the general superintendent of the Assemblies of God.

David A. Womack: I have heard you say that your campaign for revival began several years ago. What prompted that interest?

Thomas E. Trask: As I traveled to district councils and ministers institutes, the Lord allowed me to sense and see the need for a new vitality in our Fellowship. In days gone by, the Assemblies of God gave place to the person and work of the Holy Spirit. When we do that, we experience growth.

I shared this with Charles Crabtree and said, "Charles, we

need to have a holy convocation whereby we as a Pentecostal church come together to acknowledge our need of God and to ask Him to forgive us." And so he witnessed that in his spirit.

On Sunday before the Portland General Council, about four o'clock in the morning, the Holy Spirit awoke me and said, "I want you to prepare a resolution that will call for a holy convocation." (We later called it a sacred assembly.) So I did that and took the resolution to General Superintendent G. Raymond Carlson. He read it to the General Presbytery, who unanimously and enthusiastically agreed.* My burden and heartbeat is that we as a Fellowship will return to our dependence upon the work of the Spirit.

Womack: You have said that the bottom line of revival is souls being saved. Will a fresh revival in the Assemblies of God increase our burden for world missions?

Trask: I really believe that! God has blessed this Fellowship tremendously because of our emphasis on the person and work of the Holy Spirit. When we give Him place to work, He will bring to the forefront that which is closest to the heart of Christ. That's why we have missions in the Assemblies of God and why missions must remain at the forefront of this Fellowship. If the Assemblies of God ever veers from that, it's in trouble.

Womack: Did you grow up in a Pentecostal home?

Trask: I had the privilege of being raised in an Assemblies of God preacher's home. My mother and father—Waldo and Beatrice Trask—are now retired but are still active in ministry. My father was a former bartender and a butcher when he met Christ. After his conversion, he became a deacon in the local Assemblies of God church until God called him into the ministry. He never had the privilege of a Bible college education, but he had a strong dependence on the Word of God and living in the Spirit.

Womack: You say God called your father into the ministry. How can we know if God is speaking to us?

---

*The sacred assembly was held in Springfield, Missouri, on March 1–3, 1994.

Trask: We are spirit beings. I believe and was taught that as spirit beings we can live in fellowship with God. We can know the voice of the Spirit. You see, if I please the Lord and make Him part of my decision-making, then I learn to hear His voice. I am a strong advocate of what we used to teach on this subject, but you don't hear much about it anymore.

To know the will of God is not some mystery. Proverbs says, "Trust in the Lord with all thine heart; and lean not unto thine own understanding. In all thy ways acknowledge him, and he shall direct thy paths" [Proverbs 3:5–6]. If I do the first three, He will do the fourth and direct my paths. He does so through the voice of the Spirit. I call it the witness of the three *W*'s— witness of the Word, witness of circumstances, and witness of the Spirit.

Womack: Do you actually hear the voice of the Lord?

Trask: Yes. We've heard the saying that after two people have been married for a number of years they begin to look alike. Well, we have that kind of relationship with the Lord through His Spirit. If I live in the Word and in the Spirit, I then become sensitized to what the Spirit wants. There is a check when I move off to the side where I would grieve the Holy Spirit. I think that we as spiritual Christians need to be careful that we don't grieve the Spirit. The closer I get to God through fellowship with Him, prayer, and studying His Word, the more sensitized I become to His will.

I was raised in this! I had the privilege of seeing it lived out through a mom and dad who were dependent on God. Back then ministers didn't have social security, health insurance, or retirement programs in the church; and most pastors didn't make good salaries. We're all grateful for the blessings of God today, but back then ministers had to depend totally upon the Lord. They taught us to pray, to be dependent upon God. I have never gotten away from that. I don't care how affluent we might become; our dependence is upon the Holy Spirit.

Womack: Do you hear the voice of God in words?

Trask: No, it would not be in words. He witnesses. The Book of Acts records, "For it seemed good to the Holy Ghost, and to us"

[Acts 15:28].* I believe the Holy Spirit witnesses to our hearts. There is a feeling of rightness, and when it isn't right, there is a feeling of wrongness. This witness isn't only for ministers either, but for every Spirit-filled believer. John wrote, "He that hath an ear, let him hear what the Spirit saith unto the churches" [Revelation 2:7]. So the Spirit is talking! It's a matter of our being attuned. It's the fine-tuning of our spiritual dial to pick up the message that's coming from the Spirit to the churches.

I had the privilege of growing up in Sunday school and youth camps. I remember those experiences with God around the altar at camp. One of my great experiences happened at Lake Geneva Bible Camp in Minnesota. I'll never forget it, because God met me at that altar. I had just graduated from North Central Bible College and gone right into pioneering a church. A businessman had made me a very lucrative offer to go into the secular world, and the little church we were pastoring couldn't pay us anything. So I was struggling with that offer. I'll never forget that altar service as long as I live. I settled the matter that night at the altar of Lake Geneva Bible Camp, never to look back again because I knew the call of God.

Womack: Do you have that sense of rightness about being general superintendent of the Assemblies of God?

Trask: Oh, absolutely! There's not a question in my mind, and I'll tell you why. First of all, I don't believe that God desires for people to want offices. The key is to want God's will. Jesus said, "Not my will, but thine, be done" [Luke 22:42]. Jesus lived with the burning compulsion to do the will of the Father. As Christians, we must desire to live out the will of God and fulfill His purposes for our lives. God isn't impressed with titles. Jesus' ministry wasn't in titles but in towels! Servanthood! I am a servant of Jesus Christ. If He wants me to serve as a pastor, I'm happy to serve as a pastor. I love pastoring! When I was a district superintendent, I was happy as a district superintendent. When the Lord asked me to be general treasurer, all I

---

*Here we have Brother Trask's testimony of how he hears from God. Some people testify that they perceive communication from God in words or phrases. Spirit-filled individuals vary in the ways they perceive the Lord's voice speaking to them. The importance is not on the mode of perception but in knowing what God is saying.

knew was it was God's will. And I was never frustrated. I was fulfilled in the office of general treasurer because that was the will of God for my life. We don't have to strive. We just live to say, "Lord, I will fulfill Your will."

Womack: Have you served the Lord all your life?

Trask: I believed as a boy but got away from God and began my freshman year at North Central Bible College in a backslidden state. My dad put me in Bible school. He was a presbyter, and I was a rascal. He said, "I'm going to put you in Bible school, and maybe that will straighten you out." Well, it did. (When I relive some of these things, it stirs me.)

What happened was that a revival broke out, and classes were dismissed. God sovereignly moved across that student body, and for days I watched young people and professors wait before God. Hour after hour we were in the presence of God, and courses were set for people's lives. Even though I was saved as a boy in the local church and received the infilling of the Holy Spirit at youth camp, it was that revival in Bible college and the refilling with the Holy Spirit that changed my life. That's why I believe it is so important that people who have an initial experience in their youth need to have a "reexperience," a rebaptism in the Spirit, as they grow up and mature. Our experience needs to remain up-to-date and fresh in our hearts and spirits.

Womack: Can such revivals occur in our Bible colleges today?

Trask: Absolutely! I recently told the college presidents to let God move, because I know what can happen in our Bible colleges if they will have a revival. Those students will become our Pentecostal preachers.

Womack: As we think of a fresh revival in the Assemblies of God, what are some of your concerns about the local church?

Trask: One of my greatest concerns is the lack of an altar within the church, that entire area between the pulpit and the first pews. It's there that conversion takes place. It's at the altar that people meet God. It's at the altar that lives are changed. I appreciate the worship that God has brought to the church, and that's needful, but worship must never take the place of the Word or the altar. I am concerned that we have now focused our attention on worship to the exclusion of preaching. There isn't anything that can replace the preaching of the Word. We must become people of the Word; the preaching of the Word prepares us for the altar. So worship, yes—but then the Word, followed by the altar. God can climax and bring to completion what He begins earlier in the service.

At Brightmoor Tabernacle in Detroit, we were a strong church in emphasis of the Word of God. That congregation of two thousand people was never bound by time. If I preached less than forty-five minutes to an hour, they felt like they were short-changed. The people were back en masse on Sunday night. They loved the Word. Consequently, faith was alive in the congregation, and there were healings, miracles, and people being saved. This went on for years.

The Word must go forth in preaching, and then the Word must be allowed to accomplish the purpose for which it was sent. Yet, as I travel I don't see those two elements that are so needful. The worship is good, but there is a lack of emphasis on the preaching of the Word of God and then on time for the Spirit to accomplish what He wants to do at the altar. That was what brought my attention to the need for a revival in our churches.

Womack: How will you go about meeting these needs in the Assemblies of God?

Trask: I don't believe that the problems within the Assemblies of God need to be complex. When we experience a sovereign move of the Holy Spirit—a spiritual awakening within the Assemblies of God—the factors that come out of that revival will take care of the needs.

Let me give you an example. Jesus said, "But ye shall receive power, after that the Holy Ghost is come upon you: and ye shall be witnesses unto me" [Acts 1:8]. He's talking there about character, life-style. We don't have to worry about trying to legislate holiness if the life-style of the church is patterned after what the Holy Spirit would have us to be. You don't have to worry about telling Spirit-filled people they can't do this or that. I'm not interested in legislating holiness but in letting the Spirit bring conviction. In a Spirit-filled church there should come a life-style that will be pleasing to God.

Then, there will be evangelism, for we are witnesses. Evangelism will be a natural result because people will want to share what Jesus is doing in their hearts. I don't believe a person can be in fellowship with the Lord Jesus Christ without having a burden for the lost.

Womack: At the risk of impertinence, there is a question I must ask. Is your call for revival a temporary theme to be followed by something else, or should we expect this to be the central purpose of your administration?

Trask: I said it upon my installation, and I say it again: I will not rest satisfied until we see a sovereign move of the Holy Spirit in the Assemblies of God. It has nothing to do with what is popular, because I can tell you that many of the things we are touching on already are not popular out there. There are pockets of people who think it is easier to program than to pray. You have to have programs, organization, schedules, and calendars of events. I don't have any problem with that, but unless those events are Spirit-breathed and Spirit-anointed they will remain programs and will come up empty.

Some will say my call for revival is only a theme, but I can tell you of a truth that those who know what revival is and what it will do are saying, "We're with you, Brother Superintendent. We're believing with you." They know of the emptiness of a program in itself. I suppose it's going to take some time for people to know that revival for me is more than a theme. It is absolutely essential to the Assemblies of God!

I had this burden for a Pentecostal revival long before Minneapolis. And as I look back, Brother Womack, at my being elected to this office: There's no reason, no precedent, for a general treasurer being elected general superintendent—but in the providence of God. He wants revival! That isn't the heart of Thomas Trask; that's the heart of God. And it's simply a matter of aligning ourselves with what He wants. So it's okay if some stand in the shadows and just watch; God will get hold of their hearts, and they will see.

Womack: We are a very large and diversified church. As revival comes, will different churches respond differently?

Trask: I don't have any problem with what method is used as long as we all arrive at the same goal—seeing Jesus Christ glorified in the church and seeing people's lives changed. I am concerned that our churches not engage in just window-dressing the sinner, allowing people to become part of the church without any life-changing commitment to Jesus Christ. Discipleship has always required a change of life-style. Churches may have different ways of operating, but the result must be the same: believers' lives becoming effective for Jesus Christ and souls being saved.

Womack: Haven't we proved to the world that we are one of the most culturally and socioeconomically adaptable churches—that we reach into many levels of society?

Trask: Do you know why that is? It's the work of the Holy Spirit! It isn't the denomination or the structure; it's the person and the work of the Holy Spirit. He knows there is a door to every heart. If we will ask the Holy Spirit to help us find the door, He will help us reach people of many different backgrounds. He knows how to win each person to Jesus Christ. Our Lord is a God of diversity.

Womack: Someone told me you are a throwback to another time. Is that true? And, if so, what are you seeking to revive?

Trask: Church history has taught us that whenever an organization departs from its original mission, it ends up becoming a byword. The Assemblies of God was raised up to be a Pentecostal voice. I have great respect and love for the evangelical churches, but we are more than evangelical; we are Pentecostal! I look back to the years of our growth when this Fellowship was such a viable force in the world and when we allowed the Holy Spirit to guide us, empower us, and compel us. If you call that a throwback to the old, then that's exactly where I'm at because I'm coming back to what has to be the driving force of this Fellowship! We must minister through the person and work of the Holy Spirit, because that's why God raised us up!

Womack: One dictionary defines revival as "(1) an act or instance of reviving: the state of being revived: as (a) renewed attention to or interest in something; (b) a new presentation or publication of something old; (c) a period of renewed religious interest; an often highly emotional evangelistic meeting or series of meetings; (2) restoration of force, validity, or effect." Is this what you are calling for?

Trask: I suppose it encompasses all of that, but I would like the terminology for the church to be a *spiritual awakening.* I want to see an awakening to what God is wanting to do, an awakening to a life-style that is pleasing to God, an awakening to what the Spirit wants to accomplish Sunday after Sunday in our local churches, an awakening to what God is doing in the community. You see, I'm a believer that the Holy Spirit broods over a community. He can go behind walls and closed doors as the church prays. I've seen this happen. As the church becomes sensitized to what God is doing out there, it becomes the link God uses to bring people to an encounter with Jesus Christ.

Such an awakening of soul winning brings vitality and new birth to the church. It brings the life of the Spirit to the church. It may be emotional, but it doesn't have to be. I've been in services when there has been a move of God that brought a hush, and if anybody had said anything we would have felt that he or she was out of order. And then I have been in services when there has been a move of God that brought an exuberance of praise and worship. I don't want to put God in a box! I think it is a mistake to think God will always work in the same way. I think of the Jesus Movement. Nobody could have dreamed that up. That was the work of the Spirit. God sovereignly moved upon young people, and out of that came a revival known as the Jesus Movement. The churches that were spiritually alert and attuned to the Spirit embraced those young folks, and the Jesus People brought the life of Christ into the church. In other churches there was deadness, and congregations did not want that influence; so the revival just passed them by.

We have seen the divine healing emphasis, the charismatic renewal, and the latter rain. God is such a God of diversity that I don't know how He's going to choose to revive us. I must tell you, I kind of stand on tiptoes. I say, "God, what are You going to do, how are You going to do it, and where will it break out?" I just want to be in the center of the coming revival! I want the Assemblies of God to be big enough in God and open enough to God that we can say, "Whatever You want to do, just breathe upon us! Let it be fresh from Your throne!"

Womack: Are there certain things that you would expect to see in such a revival?

Trask: There will be a great hunger for the Word of God. There will be a great desire for prayer in one's life and in the church. It will result in evangelism, people being saved. Jesus said, "And I, if I be lifted up from the earth, will draw all men unto me" [John 12:32]. It will result in the miraculous taking place, because faith is a work of the Spirit. You can't have the Word and the Spirit without producing faith, and faith will produce miracles. There will be healings. Wherever you go, there will be a sense of God-consciousness, that we are walking on holy ground.

When revival happens, it focuses on the person of Jesus Christ. There is an awakening in the spirit man as a result of a hunger and a desire. If we desire Jesus, we will want to be in the house of God. It won't be a chore to go to church; we will want to go to church. That's why churches are struggling with Sunday night attendance. When God moves, we don't have to worry about people coming to church. They will be there. They will want to be there. In revival, there is a freshness of God that permeates the church atmosphere.

Womack: So revival is directly related to church growth?

Trask: There will be times when a church will go through a growth period and then level off to disciple the new converts. Then it will grow again as numbers are added into the body of Christ. I was reading Acts 4 and 5 in my devotions today, and in the midst of persecution, five thousand people were saved. That was because the church was in revival. In a true revival, people will be saved and filled with the Holy Spirit. Lives will be transformed, bodies healed, and believers encouraged. I'm not looking for something mystical; it will be so evident it will be undeniable.

Womack: In saying we are going back, we're not really talking about returning to the formation of the Assemblies of God in 1914, are we? What is it, then, that must be revived?

Trask: The Early Church! I believe, Brother Womack, that if the Assemblies of God will pattern itself after the Early Church, that's the key. The Early Church had the right ingredients. I used to have people come to me when I was pastoring, saying, "Brother Trask, should we leave our denominational church?" I would tell them that the Scripture says the Early Church "continued steadfastly in the apostles' doctrine and fellowship, and in breaking of bread, and in prayers" [Acts 2:42]. Those are the four ingredients that have to happen within the local church to make it a viable body of believers. So if those ingredients are there, a believer doesn't need to leave. But if there is no preaching of the Word of God, then it becomes a matter of spiritual survival. A person has got to get out of there to survive. And it doesn't matter to God what brand is over the door; it's a matter of living in fellowship with the Lord Jesus Christ. So the Early Church is the pattern for the Assemblies of God.

Womack: Is a revival a sovereign move of God, or is God always ready for revival and waits for us to ask?

Trask: I'm glad you brought that up because it's so vital. I believe there is balance in this. First of all, the Spirit helps us to recognize our need to draw near to God. He said, "Draw nigh to God, and he will draw nigh to you. Cleanse your hands, ye sinners; and purify your hearts, ye double-minded" [James 4:8]. The Word of God is filled with times that God used men to call a people to himself. So a God-given leader functioning under the authority of the Lord of the church will be charged with the responsibility to call people to revival. It's the responsibility of the leader to be attuned to the Head of the church, because the Head of the church is desirous of revealing himself to His church. So there are times of refreshing, times when God sovereignly moves; but there has to be the call to prayer. I don't believe that we have to move in and out of revival. A church can and should live in the spirit of revival.

Womack: Are there things about the Assemblies of God that need to change before we can experience the coming revival?

Trask: One thing that God demands is holiness. There has never been any substitute for holiness. We were known as a holiness movement, and I pray that we have not shunned that identification. We should want to please the Lord, for without holiness, the Scripture says, no man shall see God.[*] One of my

---

[*]Hebrews 12:14: "Follow peace with all men, and holiness, without which no man shall see the Lord."

28

concerns is that we remain a holiness people. Now, holiness can't be legislated; it has to be born out of relationship: I want to please the Lord, so I don't participate in the activities of the world or worldly amusements or events. I'm driven by a desire to do the things that please the Lord and this results in holiness—a life-style pleasing to God. I think that has to be preached, taught, practiced, and lived out within the church.

I saw that in my mother and father. I didn't hear one thing preached from the pulpit and see another thing lived in the home. There can't be that dichotomy. What I preach is what I live. And yet, I see evidences today of people teaching one thing on Sunday and living something else on Monday. You can't walk with the Lord on Sunday and run with the devil during the week.

Womack: I have heard it said that a real revival must begin as a grass roots movement or else it will deteriorate into a promotional campaign. Yet, revival in the Bible always started with leaders. Would you address this matter?

Trask: Well, you are right that God calls a leader. But I can show you a stack of letters from the "grass roots" saying, "Brother Trask, we recognize that God is speaking to us about revival." So I think it's both: It's leadership on a national level and on a local level. It's a witness in our spirits that this is of the Lord.

Womack: If leadership is a key to revival, what does this say about the responsibility of our pastors?

Trask: Awesome! Awesome! Again, because the pastor is the leader, he's the shepherd and is charged with the responsibility of leading his sheep to water, to pasture, to God. We dare not ever forget that. The sheep will never be any more spiritual than the shepherd.

Womack: Brother Trask, I thank you on behalf of our readers, many of whom are praying with you for revival. In our next interview I will ask you about the role of repentance in revival.

3

A Call to Repentance

A few days after our first interview, I sat again in the general superintendent's office on the third floor of the Assemblies of God Headquarters. Out the door and down the hall were the offices of the other executives, and through another door was the executive conference room with its long boardroom table. General Superintendent Thomas E. Trask sat behind his desk, and behind him was his fountain pen collection.

I turned on my voice-activated tape recorder and continued from where we had left off the first day.

David A. Womack: The other day you spoke of the awesome responsibilities of pastors. Who is responsible for revival?

Thomas E. Trask: I believe it is a general responsibility but it is also the responsibility of leaders, as in the Bible. When God raised up men, they were to become His mouthpiece and call the people to repentance. The leader must set the pace and the tone for revival.

Womack: When this revival gets started, how do you think it will affect our churches?

Trask: First, there will be such a consciousness of God in the service that unsaved people will be gripped by conviction of sin. Conviction is not only for the unsaved but also for the believer. When revival takes place, there comes a sensitivity to the sins of commission and of omission—not necessarily as a result of deliberately sinning but of failing to acknowledge or do what is right.

We can become careless in our devotional life, neglecting to read the Word of God or spend time in prayer. We can become careless in our witness or careless in our convictions. When revival comes, there will be a sharpening of our senses so that when the Holy Spirit deals with us we realign our priorities and set some new ones. This is what revival is, an awareness of the Holy Spirit dealing with our hearts and lives. The study of God's Word, daily devotions, reading the Word of God, prayer, family altar, and church attendance become a priority to us. This becomes a life-style that is pleasing to God.

Womack: You speak in many different churches. What characteristics would tell you that you are in a revived church?

Trask: There is an alive atmosphere. One of the important factors to this Fellowship is that we have had a vitality, an aliveness. I don't mean simply from singing fast choruses. I'm talking about the atmosphere being charged with the power and presence of Jesus Christ. When the unsaved come in, they find a warmth, the love of Jesus Christ abounding in that church. That life in the presence of Christ affects the song service, the prayer service, the giving, the preaching of the Word, the closing part of the service, the altar service.

With vitality comes faith. Faith is alive! There is an expectancy, an anticipation, a wonder at what is going to happen in the church service today. Jesus said, "For where two or three are gathered together in my name, there am I in the midst of them" [Matthew 18:20]. When a revived congregation is aware that Jesus is in their midst, they can expect anything to happen. The miraculous, the supernatural, the out of the ordinary take place. What happens is that it becomes God's order and not man's order. You see, we can so program the church service that we program God right out of the picture. I believe we need to plan a service, but we also need to have an openness to God. Many times I have given an altar call during the song service because the atmosphere and the conditions were such that God was speaking to the unsaved.

Womack: You place great emphasis on the altar and have said the altar service is missing in many of our churches today. Would you speak to that subject?

Trask: In the Old Testament the altar was the focal point of the temple. I believe the altar must be the centerpiece of the church and, indeed, of one's life and home. I was raised in a home where we had family altar every day. I have a son who is a senior in high school. I pray with him every morning before I leave the house. That's how people meet God. It's God's design.

I believe that in a Pentecostal church the focal point will be the altar. It's where God meets people and where the work of the Holy Spirit is accomplished. It's the climaxing of all that God has prepared the hearts to accomplish within the service. Take away the altar, and it's like a team playing in sports but never scoring. The victory is what God is wanting to accomplish.

So I'm a strong advocate of the altar. Where the pastor has placed strong emphasis on the altar, his counseling load will be lighter because the Holy Spirit can accomplish more in moments than we as people could ever do. Such times can become a changing of the nature, the character, and the spirit. When that is done by the work of the Spirit, many problems resolve themselves.

Womack: Should the pastor have an altar goal for the service?

Trask: Yes. Evangelist Kenneth Schmidt, who was known across our Fellowship and was greatly used of God, once told me, "I have never gone into a service without planning for the altar and what I want to see accomplished in that service. So if it isn't accomplished I know I missed it." I've never forgotten that, and from time to time over my years of ministry I've had to refocus and know the difference between what I was wanting to accomplish and what God was wanting to accomplish.

Womack: Healing and deliverance, speaking in tongues, manifestations of the gifts of the Spirit—will those be necessary elements in a Pentecostal revival?

Trask: I don't believe you will see a revival without those things happening. Those manifestations are evidences of the Spirit. "And these signs shall follow them that believe; In my name shall they cast out devils; they shall speak with new tongues" [Mark 16:17]. If you believe the Word, you will see the manifestations. Some people want the manifestations without the price of believing in God or walking in faith. It's the reverse! We believe and then see the manifestations. There will not be a Holy Ghost revival without these evidences. God is a supernatural God, a God of the miraculous.

Womack: And yet, are these not the very elements of a Pentecostal service that most often lead to extremes?

Trask: That's where leaders have responsibility. I believe that God gives to leaders a sense and a keen witness of what is in balance and what is out of balance—when it's of the Spirit and when it's of the flesh. And it is leadership's responsibility to (as I like to say) keep it within the banks. The river of the Holy Spirit has banks, and it is leadership's responsibility under the guidance and wisdom of God to keep the stream flowing within the proper limits. The Word of God has established the banks for us, we are not wandering and drifting and saying, "Look, I'm not sure if this is of God." The Scripture says, "The Spirit itself beareth witness with our spirit" [Romans 8:16].

Womack: We have a whole generation of young preachers and students who have never learned how to exercise this kind of control or operate in the Spirit.

Trask: Well, that is a very critical factor within the Fellowship. It needs to be role modeled so our young leaders can see that control can be exercised without quenching. I'm afraid that what has happened today, though, is that we have taken the safest route, and that is not to permit any manifestations. In so doing, however, we have robbed the church of the edification for which the manifestations of the Spirit were given.

First Corinthians 14 says that the manifestations of the Spirit are for the edifying of the body of Christ. I believe that when God designed and gave gifts to His church, He meant for them to be utilized. And if that isn't allowed to happen, how can the Body be built up? Furthermore, that belief and practice is really what sets the Pentecostal church apart from the evangelical churches. We believe in the manifestations of the gifts of the

Spirit. If the Pentecostal church doesn't allow for the manifestations of the gifts, are we Pentecostal then?

Womack: I have heard it said there is a cost to Pentecost. Is it true that repentance is required for revival?

Trask: Yes, and I will tell you why. Because it's Bible! In the Book of Revelation we read of the Spirit speaking to the seven churches, which are representative of churches today. Again and again, we find the word "repent"! We think of that word for the unsaved, but here the Spirit is speaking to the churches. It's for all of us to repent, because we are prone to failure and to shortcomings—to live after the old man. Repentance brings us back into fellowship and relationship. We must say to the Lord, "We are sorry for our coldness, our indifference, our carelessness." John wrote, "If we confess our sins, he is faithful and just to forgive us our sins, and to cleanse us from all unrighteousness" [1 John 1:9]. That's what repentance is, whether it be for sins of the flesh, sins of spirit, sins of omission, or sins of commission. Repentance is a cleansing process.

The eye is a marvelous instrument. The moment a piece of dirt hits the eye a fountain turns on, the tear duct. What does it do? It washes out the impurity. The Word says that the blood of Jesus Christ cleanses us from all sin. Just by living in the contaminants of the world I become contaminated, so I need my spirit man, my mind, and my soul cleansed. Only Jesus Christ can do that, so I come and acknowledge my need and say, "Lord, I'm sorry. Forgive me."

Womack: Is there a difference in personal, or individual, repentance and corporate repentance?

Trask: I believe that repentance starts with us as individuals. As the church, that is, corporately, we need to ask God to forgive us for our dependence upon our successes of the past. We have become proud because of our accomplishments—successes that came from God's blessing. He won't share His glory with anyone; one thing God can't stand is pride. So we must be careful as a corporate body that we never take credit for what God has done . . . and is doing. We must repent, saying, "God, we are sorry as a denomination, as a Fellowship, as the Assemblies of

God, if we have become proud, self-sufficient, and arrogant. Forgive us, Lord!"

Womack: How do we convince slumbering and neglectful Christians of their need for repentance?

Trask: Well, first we must come back to preaching the Word of God. I can hammer on people and never accomplish a thing, but I can preach the Word accompanied by the Spirit and it will become a hammer. One of my concerns for our Fellowship is that we have left off preaching the Word.

Pentecostal preaching of the Word cannot be accomplished in a twenty-minute Sunday morning sermon. One of the dangers that I see in the Assemblies of God is this: We are taking forty-five minutes to worship and fifteen minutes for the Word. It should be fifteen minutes for worship and forty-five minutes in the Word, because faith results from the Word. "So then faith cometh by hearing, and hearing by the word of God" [Romans 10:17]. Faith comes out of the work of the Spirit through the Word of God.

The more I study the Word the more that Book becomes alive to my spirit. So let the Spirit work through the Word, because if all we are going to do is stir the emotions, then when people hit a crisis they don't have any foundation or footing. When the Word of God is given in balance, we have people who are in balance. So that's the challenge.

Womack: If we are encouraging repentance, are we not also opening a door for negative thinking?

Trask: I'm not afraid of the negative because that's the far extreme to one side, and then you can have the far extreme to the other side. So the extremes are a good check and balance for keeping the majority in the moderate middle. We just have to be careful that we don't let the skeptics come with their unbelief and kill what God is wanting to do.

Womack: Does the biblical idea of repenting in sackcloth and ashes carry with it the thought of loosening or even releasing our ties to material things as revival comes?

Trask: I don't believe there is anything wrong with the church having material things; wealth and material blessing come from the Lord. It's when the material things have the church that we are in trouble. Now I must say that for many people it's difficult, because when they acquire material goods they lose the priority of management and stewardship of the things of God. And it's the same way with the church. Believers must understand stewardship and ownership, that these things God has given us are not ours but only lent to us.

Womack: If we have a large-scale response to this call to repentance in the Assemblies of God, what do we do next?

Trask: Following repentance, there will come a hunger for God. You see, the promises of God are contingent—"If my people, which are called by my name, shall humble themselves, and pray, and seek my face, and turn from their wicked ways; then will I hear from heaven, and will forgive their sin, and will heal their land" [2 Chronicles 7:14]. All the promises of God are contingent upon our humbling ourselves, praying, seeking God's face, and turning from our wicked ways. If we do those things— "then will I . . . ," says the Lord. So once we have taken care of the cleansing process that comes with repentance, then we can expect to hear from heaven. Now as I see it, that is a life-style, not just a onetime repentance; because, as I have said, we live in a contaminated world and become contaminated just by the fact that we have to rub elbows with the world. But after we move toward God and allow our spirits to be open to the things of God, study His Word and seek His face, then we will begin to see the hand of God move toward us.

Womack: Some of the roots of the Pentecostal movement are in A. B. Simpson and the Holiness movement. Are we still part of that movement?

Trask: We had better be! Because without holiness no man shall see God. Now I believe this, that holiness and the degree of holiness is related to relationship. My relationship with the Lord Jesus Christ is going to determine my life-style. We are a church that is a strong proponent of the Christian life-style, of living out the work and life of Christ. That's why in Acts 1:8 Jesus said, "But ye shall receive power, after that the Holy Ghost is come upon you: and ye shall be witnesses unto me." *Be* witnesses of Christ! That means living the life-style of Jesus Christ, living out His life-style of holiness. The closer we get to Jesus, the more of His life we will represent. It won't be a matter of you can't do this or you can't do that. We have gone through that and, very frankly, in years gone by we have lost generations because we were so dogmatic on the "don'ts." I am more convinced of the "won'ts." I won't want to do anything that displeases the Lord. It isn't a matter of "I can't." I won't want to sin because of my relationship with the Lord Jesus Christ. A revival will produce a holy people.

Womack: I have heard it said that we believe in both instantaneous and progressive sanctification—that we are made clean at salvation but then must learn to live the Christian life. Do we sometimes demand too much too soon of new converts?

Trask: Years ago we used to have the old membership cards. If you didn't do this and this, you could be a member of an Assemblies of God church. We were legislating holiness. We had people who wanted to be members but did not yet have the relationship with Jesus Christ to make that possible. God has to change the nature, change the character.

Let me identify one example—smoking. A man gets saved and wants to rid himself of the smoking habit, and yet he might be so bound that try as hard as he might he can't do it in himself. But we would stick a membership card under his nose right after he gets saved and say, "If you want to be a member of the Assemblies of God church you have to quit smoking"—a response we legislated. We must realize that the church doesn't deliver people; God delivers them! And the marvelous part is that the Holy Spirit does the convicting, which means I shouldn't be going around saying you shouldn't be doing this or that. But when the Holy Spirit convicts them, they have to deal with the Holy Spirit. The result is that the Holy Spirit has the same standard for the entire Church.

Womack: Yet, are there not some things that a born-again, Spirit-filled Christian will not do?

Trask: Oh, absolutely! Many things. Let me give you an example. I don't think that a person filled with the Holy Ghost will look at pornography. It isn't pleasing to God because it is a gratification of the flesh produced by lust. Some years ago pornography was not as prevalent or readily available as it is today. We seldom had to deal with the problem of pornography; so we might not have had it on any list. If we were to establish such a list, we would have to keep adding to it as the enemy brought along new devices and new inventions. That's why we dare not establish the list but leave that to the work of the Holy Spirit.

Yes, there will be evidences of a holy separation from the world in a revived church. When people find Jesus and come into new life in Christ, you will hear it again and again that they no longer do this or that—not because the church told them they couldn't do it but because they don't want to do it.

Womack: And isn't it true also that when revival comes there will be some things that may not be wrong in themselves but become a matter of priority?

Trask: We begin to look at things not through our eyes anymore but through the eyes of the Holy Spirit. That's a marvelous truth, because when God removes the eye scales from our eyes and we begin to see as the Spirit sees, then our priorities come into proper place. That's why James, speaking of prayer, said, "A double-minded man is unstable in all his ways" [James 1:8]. Later in his epistle, James said, "Ye ask, and receive not, because ye ask amiss, that ye may consume it upon your lusts" [James 4:3]. It means that either we can pray in the will of God or we can pray to consume upon self. That's also true of a person's life-style. When we have experienced a revival in our spirit man and God has given us priorities that are listed by Him and not by the church, our lives will be changed.

Womack: What would you say to a pastor who wants revival in his church?

Trask: Revival won't come without prayer, so the first thing I would say to him is to establish a prayer ministry within the church. Now there might be various prayer ministries going on, but on this matter of revival I think we all need to come together, we need to zero in, for the sake of praying for revival. So I would encourage the pastor to call his people to prayer.

I would encourage him also to establish days of fasting. I'm a strong proponent of fasting. Today's church has not utilized the benefit of fasting as we did in days gone by because we are so prone to consumption and the gratification of the flesh. But there is strong, strong admonition in the Word to fast. Fasting and praying and waiting upon God—we're not good at these anymore. We are so programmed with a fast-food mentality that we want God to immediately dish it up. Or maybe we have had so much blessing, and it has come so easily for us, that we are not willing to wait for anything that will require some diligence on our part.

I would encourage the pastor to begin to preach on revival, to answer the question, What is revival? Most people in our congregations don't have the slightest idea of what we are talking about. I am not speaking about revival meetings but a whole new spiritual awakening. Let there begin to grow a hunger as a result of the Spirit mixing that word with faith and desire.

Then I would keep reporting to the people the revivals that are happening today. That creates hunger in our hearts. I just heard a report of great revival in one of the South American countries. I recently sat down with the superintendent of the Assemblies of God in Cuba and was told how they had quadrupled their Decade of Harvest goals in the first three years of the nineties. Program? No, *revival!* I said to him, "You pray with us that the winds of revival will blow across those waters and come up our coast and sweep across America!"

The Scripture admonishes, "Remember therefore from whence thou art fallen, and repent, and do the first works; or else I will come unto thee quickly, and will remove thy candlestick out of his place, except thou repent" [Revelation 2:5]. The Lord says to remember, repent, return!

Womack: Isn't a major purpose of fasting to give priority and concentration to prayer?

Trask: You can't manipulate God through fasting. It must be understood that the things I have stated are not for manipulation of God but to bring us back into His favor. We must understand that. Fasting is for our sake!

Womack: What do you wish to say to people in Assemblies of God leadership?

Trask: I believe that leaders must set the example, set the tone. That's why God puts people into leadership. So my first desire is that we would see a sovereign move of the Holy Spirit in this family right here at the Assemblies of God Headquarters. As that happens, then it will spread out across the Fellowship. We need revival desperately! Our effectiveness is going to be measured by how spiritual we are, not by how many tools we have, not by how many gadgets, not by our cleverness, nor by our human wisdom, but as a result of how close we are to fulfilling the mandate of God.

Womack: What do you say to our evangelists?

Trask: I tell evangelists: "Brethren, go to our churches with a fresh word from God and believe God to use you in an apostolic ministry." That's the purpose of evangelists, to stir up the church. Now you can't do that if you are just using the same set of sermons over and over again; every local church is a particular entity and has particular needs. God knows how to open that body to revival and to stir that body. If you use the same formula, the same recipe, every place you go, that becomes repetition. For a fresh stirring, the Word of God has to be fresh in our hearts.

If evangelists will lead the church in prayer and believe God for the miraculous, seek God for a fresh message for the congregation, and allow the gifts of the Spirit to operate, revival will take place. Evangelists must go there with a burden for the lost, and pray for the lost.

Years ago, when I was in pastoral ministry, I had evangelists who wanted to go out during the day to invite people to the church. There has to be a burden. I've said to the evangelists to go there with a burden. Let there be a compassion of God upon their hearts and lives.

Womack: What would you like to say to our Bible colleges?

Trask: I have said to our college presidents, "Please help us in insisting that the faculty in our colleges be Pentecostal." I'm not talking about being Pentecostal in doctrine only but in experience and practice. Those teachers are role models!

I was teaching a class in one of our colleges, and I asked, "How many of you have ever been in a revival—not revival meetings but a sovereign move of the Holy Spirit?" In a class of about forty students preparing for the ministry, only seven raised their hands. We're going to produce ministers who have no idea of what we are talking about. What makes my heart yearn for revival, Brother Womack, is what I experienced in Bible college.

Womack: You have told us about the revival that changed your life in Bible college. Where else have you seen revival?

Trask: We experienced it in Vicksburg, Michigan. We went to a little community of seventeen hundred people where the church had only about twenty people. The district superintendent said, "When you go there you'll feel like either staying or running." It was one of those tough, tough places. God spoke to our hearts that this was the place for us to minister. We began to pray and get the people to pray. God sent a move of the Holy Spirit that touched that community, and the church went to 250.

We experienced revival at Saginaw, Michigan. The church of about 150 had gone through a split, and the people who were left were depressed and disheartened. I said, "Look, we're not going to worry about where some people have gone. We're going to believe God for a move of the Holy Spirit." I watched God sovereignly move, and His Spirit lay like a cloud over that Saginaw Valley. It was so effortless to see people saved, healed, and filled with the Holy Ghost week after week after week. This went on for years.

I also experienced revival in my last pastorate, Brightmoor Tabernacle in Detroit, one of our historic churches. I had been serving as superintendent of the Michigan District, and I wrestled with God whether I should leave the district office and go back to pastoring. My agreement with God was, "I will go to Brightmoor Tabernacle if that's what you want me to do. I have only one request and that is that You give us revival."

I'm not geared for the status quo. I'm just not programmed that way. Some men are comfortable to go through the form of service after service, week after week, and never see people saved or anything spiritual happen. I knew this church had peaked numerically and that for all practical purposes was in the inner city. It evidently was on its way down, and I didn't want to be a part of that. But God assured me that if I would be obedient He would give us revival. He did, and the church began

41

to grow. It went from nine hundred to twenty-two hundred people over those years, and it was effortless as people were being saved, filled with the Holy Ghost, and healed. It was marvelous!

So I know what God will do and that there isn't an Assemblies of God church in America that cannot experience revival if the pastor and people will follow the admonition of the Word of God. There is no secret formula for revival!

Womack: Many of us were raised on the idea that a spirit of revival is absolutely essential for a Pentecostal church.

Trask: I believe it! I believe what happened in those local churches has to happen for the whole fellowship of the Assemblies of God. We have been a revival movement, and to move away from that will spell death. Let me put it this way: We were birthed as a revival movement, and we must stay a revival movement! We have moved away, but God hasn't moved!

Womack: As with the churches you pastored and where I saw revival in Bogotá, Colombia, and Twin Palms Assembly of God in San Jose, California, there are other local churches with spiritual pastors and praying people who are in revival right now. Yet their numbers are small. Don't we need a fresh outpouring of the Holy Ghost that will affect the whole Pentecostal movement?

Trask: That's what God is doing and will do! The present revivals are evidence, you see. The prophet asked, "Do you see rain?" On the seventh look, his servant finally came back and said, "Behold, there ariseth a little cloud out of the sea, like a man's hand" [1 Kings 18:44]. There came a great rain that revived the land.

Womack: Brother Trask, I thank you for your openness in sharing your vision for revival in the Assemblies of God.

4

The Fire and the Fellowship

It has ever been true that religious people find it difficult to maintain a high level of spiritual intensity. Consequently, as a movement grows, a revelation of God that began in a blaze of glory will fade to a popular level of somewhat lesser devotion, and with the passing of generations it loses its sense of wonder and its singleness of purpose.

How, then, does God keep the flame alive from one age to another? It is here that we must realize the solemn truth that death and resurrection are essential aspects of our religion. The same Children of Israel who murmured at the bitter waters of Marah later experienced the glory of Mount Sinai. The sons of the frightened people who backed away from the Promised Land at Kadesh became the bright-eyed warriors who crossed the Jordan on dry land and miraculously conquered Jericho. Not every individual will understand the ways of the Lord, but in each era God will raise up a people to accomplish His will. He will offer revival, and those who respond will go forward in His name in a new blaze of glory.

Let's put it this way: If the Lord should tarry in His coming, in the twenty-first century He will have a people who will proclaim His gospel. The question is not whether that revival will occur but whether we will be a part of it. God is not in crisis; it is we who are in crisis, at a crossroads deciding if we will dedicate ourselves to a Pentecostal revival or back away and wander in the lowlands of a lesser commitment.

A Key to Revival

Donald Gee, an early Pentecostal writer and camp meeting speaker, said, "One of the things I find in the modern revival is a great tendency to get the congregation happy. The modern evangelist wants to get everyone singing and smiling, and the general slogan seems to be 'Everybody happy?' He drills the congregation in this until everyone shouts, 'Amen!' If I understand the Bible, a real revival begins by making everyone unhappy. The mighty revivals of our fathers' days used to make congregations weep instead of laugh. No, I am afraid we are suffering from too much shallowness."

People tend to see a revival as a series of enthusiastic meetings rather than a spiritual awakening. A true revival, however, makes a lasting impression on a church or individual. A revival is not a mere state of mind but a quality of relationship to God himself.

In one of the clearest revival formulas in Scripture, James said, "Submit yourselves therefore to God. Resist the devil, and he will flee from you. Draw nigh to God, and he will draw nigh to you. Cleanse your hands, ye sinners; and purify your hearts, ye double-minded. Be afflicted, and mourn, and weep: let your laughter be turned to mourning, and your joy to heaviness. Humble yourselves in the sight of the Lord, and he shall lift you up" (James 4:7–10).

This is a simple principle: If we submit ourselves to God and resist the devil, God will draw nearer to us and the devil will remain at a distance. On the other hand, if we yield to the devil and resist God, the devil will be nearby and we will be far from God. This being the case, the Lord calls out to us as sinners and double-minded people to wash our hands, purify our hearts, let our laughter be turned to mourning and our joy to heaviness, and humble ourselves. Only then will He lift us up or revive us. Lest we be tempted to assign that admonition to unbelievers, we must remind ourselves that James wrote those words to Christian "brethren" (James 1:2; 2:1; 3:10).

History, like beauty, is in the eye of the beholder. In the following pages we offer a summary of Pentecostal church history. It will differ from the viewpoints of most church history books because they were written without the benefit of a Pentecostal experience and perspective. This is how we Pentecostals see it—

that the Early Church lost something vital to aggressive, evangelistic Christianity and did not regain it until this century. That *something* certainly includes the experience of the baptism in the Holy Spirit with speaking in other tongues, but it is more: It is a holy return to the beliefs, experiences, practices, and priorities of New Testament Christianity as founded by Jesus Christ and taught by His apostles. At the core of every true Pentecostal believer is a deep respect for original Christianity as experienced by the first Christians and given to us in the New Testament.

Some will say that we have left something out of this overview and others that we went too far, but this synopsis is intended only to show some general trends that demonstrate our need of a fresh anointing of the Holy Spirit to revive us once again. We do not question here the church's organization, administration, programs, or social functions but assume that in every age the church has organized itself to carry out its goals and adapted its methods to reach the people of its time and culture. Rather, we question the church's spirituality, righteousness, and dedication to God and His Holy Word.

Our Pentecostal Roots

The Pentecostal movement did not begin in the twentieth century but on the Day of Pentecost in A.D. 30, when the 120 were "all filled with the Holy Ghost, and began to speak with other tongues, as the Spirit gave them utterance" (Acts 2:4). At the first altar call, three thousand people accepted Jesus Christ as their Savior. Peter said, "Repent, and be baptized every one of you in the name of Jesus Christ for the remission of sins, and ye shall receive the gift of the Holy Ghost" (Acts 2:38). All three thousand were saved, baptized in water, and filled with the Holy Spirit on the Day of Pentecost. From that day forward, the church grew rapidly across the Roman Empire and beyond. Yet, with time and new generations, there came problems that caused the church to lose its first love (Revelation 2:4).

What were some of the problems that caused the postapostolic church to lose its Pentecostal nature? First, the church was scattered. It was a long time before anyone outside Galatia could read a copy of Paul's Epistle to the Galatians or before believers in Asia Minor could read his Epistle to the Romans.

Few Christians saw more than one of the four Gospels, and many did not see any of the writings that would eventually become part of the New Testament. A deterioration of the faith was inevitable as Christianity spread. By the time the New Testament canon was established, the church already had wandered far from the original pattern.

Second, methods of transportation were so slow and communications so limited that churches in different areas developed along separate lines, eventually forming the Coptic, Armenian, Syrian, Greek Orthodox, Roman Catholic, and other churches. This scattering of Christians without the guidance of a full and available New Testament was detrimental to the body of Christ.

The Dark Ages truly lived up to their name, for the Bible had become inaccessible to the common people, cloistered away in isolated monasteries and libraries. Only with Gutenberg's invention of the printing press about midfifteenth century did people have any opportunity to read God's Word for themselves, and even then the first Bibles were in Latin. Soon thereafter, Martin Luther translated the Bible into German, William Tyndale put it into English, and other translations appeared throughout Europe. The return of the Bible caused an immediate revolution, more kindly called the Reformation, because the church of that day had little in common with that described in the New Testament. From the time the Bible was restored to the hands of the people, the church has been returning step by step to the biblical pattern of original Christianity.

In the last half of the nineteenth century, there came an emphasis on the difference between claiming to be a Christian and living up to biblical standards. A. B. Simpson was one of the best-known leaders of what was called the Holiness movement. Some church historians would include Dwight L. Moody and Charles G. Finney in that movement. Many of the Holiness people came out of mainline churches that had turned to a liberal theology, called modernism. Within the Holiness movement an interest in the person and work of the Holy Spirit as described in the New Testament was increasing.

At a small Bible school in Topeka, Kansas, a group of students who did not go home for Christmas sought God in prayer and supplication for ten days as the first believers had done leading up to the Day of Pentecost. Ten days later, on New Year's Day of 1901, they were all filled with the Holy Spirit and spoke in other tongues just as on the Day of Pentecost. That mighty explosion of dynamic spiritual power could not be contained in Topeka and soon spread to Kansas City and around the country. Beginning in 1906 on Azusa Street in Los Angeles, there was a wonderful move of God that brought the new Pentecostal movement to the attention of the church world. Most of today's Pentecostal churches trace their origins to the Azusa Street revival.

Charles T. Crabtree, assistant general superintendent of the Assemblies of God, wrote in his book *The Pentecostal Priority,* "From the beginning of the outpouring at Topeka, Kansas, the Pentecostal phenomena incited a New Testament reaction. Church annals of the first decades of the twentieth century are filled with accounts of powerful ministries, miracles of God, intense persecution, generosity in sharing material goods, intercessory prayer, and fellowship. It was almost a repeat of the occurrences recorded in the Book of Acts. And the Lord added to the church daily."

For the most part, the religious world rejected the new Pentecostals and dismissed them from its churches. For a time even fellow Christians in the Holiness movement declared that speaking in tongues was of the devil, and people who did not understand the power of Pentecostal altar services called Pentecostals "holy rollers"—a term we Pentecostals have never seriously denied and may even hold in guarded respect. Many people were drawn to our meetings and found personal salvation, the baptism in the Holy Spirit, miraculous answers to prayer, and warm Christian fellowship. Some came out of the dim light of spiritually cold churches, and many unchurched were saved from the darkness of sin in response to our ardent evangelism. People who knew their Bibles well associated the new movement with original Christianity and flocked to join us.

In April 1914, the General Council of the Assemblies of God was formed at Hot Springs, Arkansas—called there because it was central in the country and was on a railroad line. What that call was to is defined in the opening statement of the first official minutes of that meeting: "For a number of years, God has been leading men to seek for a full apostolic gospel standard of experience and doctrine." We have never improved on that definition because our founders understood that the Pentecostal movement was a return to original, New Testament, apostolic,

Pentecostal Christianity—that it was not a cult but the very core of Christianity!

George O. Wood, general secretary of the Assemblies of God, said,

> The prophet Joel talked about the early and latter rains (2:23). The early rains of October and November were to soften the parched ground so that seed could be sown. But, the latter rains of April were also needed to ripen the fruit and stay the drought of the long, dry summer. The latter rain was directly related to the ripening of the harvest.
>
> Looking back on this twentieth century, we can see the early rains of Topeka, Kansas; Azusa Street in Los Angeles; and Hot Springs, Arkansas. This was the softening of the ground for the planting of the end-time harvest. Now, we're at the conclusion of this century and millennium. I have felt the Holy Spirit saying to me, "Azusa Street was only a shower compared to what I purpose to do in the days yet ahead." The greater harvest is yet to come. That's why the rain is needed!
>
> Pentecost, both as an Old Testament festival and a New Testament observance, is directly linked to the harvest. We seek a new Pentecost in our hearts, not simply from a desire to have a more illumined inner experience with God. The experience of Pentecost can never be separated from the completion of the harvest. God pours out His Spirit so that the harvest of the earth may be made ripe. With revival comes great evangelism. Indeed, there can be no revival if only the church is revived, for a revived church results in an evangelized community.

With the rebirth of the New Testament church, our Pentecostal forefathers began to see New Testament results. Many people were saved from their sins, healed of their sicknesses, delivered from evil, and guided by the Holy Spirit. The worship was enthusiastic; prayers were out loud; the preaching style was fervent, powerful, and effective; and what happened at the altar had not been seen since the Early Church. The experience of the baptism in the Holy Spirit with its evidence of speaking in other tongues had revolutionized the church and restored the original concept of direct evangelism of the world. In the second General Council, Lemuel C. Hall framed a resolution calling for "the greatest evangelism that the world has ever seen."

A major factor in the twentieth-century Pentecostal awakening was an expectation of the imminent return of Jesus Christ.

Believing strongly that biblical prophecies call for the rapture of the Church followed by an outpouring of God's wrath on the world, the early Pentecostals spread the gospel as quickly and as far as they could. The fire of the baptism in the Holy Spirit, combined with this sense of prophetic urgency, was the driving force behind the movement. There were many cottage prayer meetings, church services had no announced dismissal time, crowds came to church on Sunday night, sermons were seldom shorter than forty-five minutes, and altar services often continued into the night.

Problems in Paradise

However, in time there were problems. A people who lived along the outer limits of human emotion and intuition were certain to face temptations in the very areas of their greatest strengths; so they always ran the risk of emotion for its own sake and of unwise practices intended to keep the feelings at a high pitch. As a result, more attention might have been given to human experience than to divine revelation. Yet, God led us successfully through those years. In fact, many of us today would rather deal with what we used to call wildfire than with the dull embers of today's cooler and more proper churches. When will we realize that we always have grown best in the highly charged atmosphere of a full Pentecostal commitment? Far from driving people away, an environment of deep devotion, trust in spiritual phenomena, and unbridled response to the Spirit attracts people by the multitudes! Yes, in our enthusiasm we sometimes went too far on the side of human feelings, but certain extremes may be a price to pay for attaining a higher general revival. In other words, there may be no revival without a broad range of behavior and ideas.

By the twenties, the Assemblies of God was becoming more organized, Bible schools were training ministers, missionaries were spreading the gospel over the earth, and everywhere people were coming to Christ. However, our very growth was becoming a problem to us. As our Movement became popular, it became more categorized, more limited to written explanations, and more apt to refer to doctrine rather than personal experience. Such a watering down of the very things that bring a movement into being will contribute to its eventual decline and demise.

Another problem that threatened to slow down the Movement was its level of ministerial education. In the beginning, many of our pastors were trained ministers who had been filled with the Holy Spirit and had come from other denominations. Unfortunately, many of them erroneously concluded that higher education was detrimental to Pentecostal ministry: If the inspiration for anointed preaching came from the Lord, then education or even detailed sermon preparation might get in the way of hearing from Him. They based such a response on a misinterpretation of Psalm 81:10, "Open thy mouth wide, and I will fill it." As a result, many people entered the ministry with little preparation and tended to emphasize shallow "clothesline preaching" about cultural mores rather than the deeper truths of Christian morality. We must not forget, however, that they were the very people who made many converts and laid the foundation upon which our supposedly wiser generation is attempting to build! Yet, over the years we have learned that God does not pour His message through the preacher like water through a funnel but rather draws from the anointed minister's storehouse of knowledge, experience, and preparation. The holy anointing does not descend upon the Spirit-filled preacher only while he delivers his sermons but rests upon his entire life and life-style . . . in his personal living, behind the pulpit, and during his private hours of devotion and sermon preparation. We paid for failing to understand the nature of Spirit-anointed ministry with intense but shallow preaching, which majored on exterior standards rather than interior principles of righteousness.

Challenges to Our Faith

There is no need here to go into a detailed history. The problems we faced were natural results of revival, and in the coming revival we will experience them once again. We will have a renewed enthusiasm, emotional services, and the leadership of fiery-eyed fanatics, like Paul, Peter, and Stephen—men who gave their lives for the cause. (Indeed, we expect to be among them!) The challenge will be to keep the Movement biblical. When we call for a revival, we are not suggesting a simple formula of man-made refurbishments by organization or program; we are crying out to God for Him to take over our lives and restore us to His will and His way. We have no idea how God will do it or what forms it may take; we can only raise our voices and say, "Thus saith the Lord!"

One of the temptations of Jesus was that He put His Father's power on display, that He leap from the pinnacle of the temple. The temptation was to make a show of trusting in God's miraculous power. We confronted the same temptation in the great healing meetings of the forties and fifties. There were many sincere men and women of God who had powerful healing campaigns, but their successes led others with other motives to emulate them. What was intended as God's miraculous accompaniment to soul winning was sometimes put on display as an end in itself.

In Mark 16:15–18, miraculous signs were to follow those who would go into all the world and preach the gospel. Biblical divine healing always is found along the cutting edge of evangelism. Let us be careful here, for the line must be drawn short of showmanship without sacrificing successful mass evangelism, where the Lord often has blessed convert making with supernatural healings and deliverance. Yet, how often we have learned sad lessons when we have paraded the intimate things of God before the ungodly without properly proclaiming the gospel! From the old tent healing campaigns to modern television, we have been at our worst when we have tried to show off God's mighty power in a setting unworthy of such holy manifestations of glory. Such misuses of spiritual power have had a backlash: turning many of our pastors and churches away from trust in the miraculous.

We also met the challenge of the Latter Rain movement, which had much to commend it but carried the gifts of the Spirit to unscriptural extremes. Ironically, our biggest problem with the Latter Rain movement came after we had dealt with what they taught and practiced—we turned away from the operation of the gifts of the Spirit altogether.

Another mixture of challenge and blessing was the charismatic movement. A good case can be made for the idea that the mid-century charismatic renewal among the old-line denominations was a direct outgrowth of the Pentecostal movement earlier in the century. At the same time, there is a difference between charismatic and Pentecostal. Pentecostals may be called charismatic, but charismatics are not necessarily Pentecostal. To be charismatic is to identify with a revival of belief and acceptance of the charismatic gifts of the Spirit, as listed in 1 Corinthians 12:1–11. To be Pentecostal is to identify with the birth of the whole Church on the Day of Pentecost, including being in one accord in God's house, being filled with the Holy Spirit, speaking in other tongues, explaining the prophecies of the Scriptures, preaching the gospel to the masses, making an altar call to bring them to repentance, practicing water baptism, leading converts into the same spiritual experience as the apostles in being filled with the Holy Spirit, and continuing in the apostles' doctrine. The Pentecostal movement refers to the whole life of the church, while being charismatic applies only to certain aspects of church life.

And yet, rather than exercising the wisdom of waiting for the Holy Spirit to do His work, many Pentecostals were wary of the revival and expected newly Spirit-filled people to believe and act just like themselves. At first the charismatic Christians tried to remain in their traditional denominations, but with time they were dissatisfied there and began to form their own churches. They then experienced many of the same extremes that we knew early in our Movement.

Our relationship to the charismatic movement produced three notable effects upon us. First, we withdrew from participation in the charismatic movement, thereby cutting ourselves off from influencing some of the people in it. Two men who tried to call us to ministry to the charismatic movement were Donald Gee and David duPlessis, both of whom may have been ahead of their times. (That failure to accept the charismatic challenge may be one of the reasons for our present lack of growth.)

Second, in the United States the Assemblies of God was the fastest-growing denomination in the decade of the eighties. Our growth was inflated because of the influx of charismatic people into our numbers. This rapid growth masked the fact that our convert growth from among the unchurched had decreased. We must learn to distinguish between the primary evangelism of making converts, the secondary evangelism of leading our own children to Christ, and the tertiary evangelism of drawing people from other churches.

The third problem resulting from our relationship with the charismatic movement is more difficult to identify. One aspect of the movement was its revival of open praise. This was wonderful and provided us with an emphasis that we needed. However, in adopting charismatic methods many of our pastors and their churches abandoned Pentecostal worship styles in favor of the more socially acceptable charismatic methods. One notable example is that charismatic praise is largely a group activity, while Pentecostal altar services focus intensely on the needs and life changes of the individual. (We will explore Pentecostal worship more in a later chapter.)

Spirit-filled people often have a problem interpreting what God is saying to them. What we first interpreted as the approaching doom of the Great Tribulation turned out to be the horrors of World War I. In the early thirties many Pentecostal people thought the Lord would come in 1936, followed by the outpouring of God's wrath, the Antichrist, and Armageddon. Although the Lord did not come, World War II nearly fulfilled those expectations. More recently, many of us saw prophetic meaning in the events in the Persian Gulf War, and yet the war (at least temporarily) ended. For other major events, such as the breakup of the Soviet Union, our prophets were strangely silent until after the fact.

Rather than trying to identify the Antichrist or superimpose contemporary events on the Scriptures, we must recognize that the single most important Bible prophecy about our times is in Matthew 24:14, where Jesus said, "And this gospel of the kingdom shall be preached in all the world for a witness unto all nations; and then shall the end come." The "end" of which Jesus spoke in this passage, according to verses 30–31, is the end of this age at the rapture of the Church, followed by the mourning of the tribes of the earth in the Day of Wrath—the same scenario we may trace through the Book of Revelation.

Consider this literal translation of Matthew 24:14—"And this good news of the kingdom will be proclaimed in the whole inhabited earth, resulting in a witness to every ethnic society; and then the end will have come."[*] According to Jesus, the Church will accomplish its Great Commission of preaching the gospel to "every creature" (Mark 16:15). The Church will not go down in defeat at the last but will complete its calling with great enthusiasm and success . . . indeed in a final revival!

---

[*]Translation by David A. Womack.

This is what we are feeling, this prophetic calling to the Church to rise up and do what it was called to do. It is every bit as Spirit-spoken as any prophecy ever delivered in our churches. The end of this age is approaching, Jesus is coming, and we must both prepare ourselves and proclaim the good news to the world.

What Do We Do Now?

A century of living as Pentecostal people has produced a complicated and highly structured church that is as likely to change as the ancient Jews were on the morning of the Day of Pentecost. Yet, by nine o'clock that morning the winds of the Spirit had blown, tongues of fire had come down from heaven, and the 120 were filled with the Holy Spirit and were speaking in other tongues. Peter preached the first Pentecostal sermon without notes, and by the end of that day three thousand traditional religious people had been transformed into fervent Christians ready to lay down their lives for Jesus Christ.

We can change! God can break through our traditions and routines and revive us! The question is, What should we do?

The answer is so simple that you'll wonder why you had to read all these pages to get to it. It's so rudimentary that you may not do it because you will suspect that it is not enough, that perhaps God requires some greater or more outstanding effort from you. However, if revival could be started by human effort, we probably would have done so already. Why not accept and follow God's plan?

Are you ready? Here it is: Join in one accord in prayer and supplication.

Ten days before Pentecost, Christ's followers gathered in the Upper Room. In Acts 1:13–14, Luke listed the disciples (minus Judas Iscariot) and referred to certain women with "Mary the mother of Jesus, and with his brethren." He then said, "These all continued with one accord in prayer and supplication." Within a few days their number had grown to 120, so we must assume they had moved the prayer meetings to the temple courtyard, where ten days later "they were all filled with the Holy Ghost, and began to speak with other tongues, as the Spirit gave them utterance" (Acts 2:4).

The solution is simple . . . so do it!

R. A. Torrey said,

I can give a prescription that will bring revival to any church or community or any city on earth. First, let a few Christians (they need not be many) get thoroughly right with God themselves. This is the prime essential. If this is not done, the rest that I am to say will come to nothing.

Second, let them bind themselves together in a prayer group to pray for a revival so that God opens the heavens and comes down.

Third, let them put themselves at the disposal of God for Him to use as He sees fit in winning others to Christ. That is all!

This is sure to bring a revival to any church or community. I have given this prescription around the world. It has been taken by many churches and many communities, and in no instance has it ever failed; and it cannot fail!

5

Revivals in the Bible

The word *revival* does not appear in the Bible, although the Word of God does include the verbs "revive," "revived," and "reviving." In the New Testament, "revived" is used twice—once that sin revived (Romans 7:9) and once that Christ died and revived (Romans 14:9). There were no revivals in the New Testament because the first Christians had experienced something never known before the Day of Pentecost. By the end of the first century, some had left their first love (Revelation 2:4), but there is no indication that they ever repented and were revived.

When people strayed from the truth in Old Testament times, God first issued a call to repentance by the voices and pens of His prophets. In most cases neither the people nor their leaders listened to such messengers but continued their sinful ways until God's judgment fell upon them. Only in retrospect were the prophets respected.

We must recognize that in the Bible revivals occurred only when a spiritual awakening began with the leaders! Therein lies the significance of this call to revival. Over the years many prophetic preachers and writers have called us to prayer and repentance, but now the word is coming from the leaders of our church. General Superintendent Thomas E. Trask came into office calling for revival in the Assemblies of God, and he is supported and encouraged by his fellow officers: Assistant General Superintendent Charles T. Crabtree, General Secretary George

O. Wood, General Treasurer James K. Bridges, and the other nonresident executive and district officers. These men have heard from heaven and will lead this Fellowship into a fresh revival if we will repent of our sins and return to God.

In his installation to office in the inauguration ceremony at the Assemblies of God Headquarters chapel on November 18, 1993, General Superintendent Trask said, "I promise not to rest content with any measure of numerical growth until the Assemblies of God has experienced a sovereign move of the Holy Spirit that will result in a Pentecostal revival that touches every church in this great Fellowship."

Let there be no question about it: The coming revival will begin when the leaders, from general superintendent to district officers to sectional presbyters to local pastors, fall on their knees in repentance before God and then lead in the ways of the Spirit rather than in the ways of men. Once that revival occurs, the people of our churches will follow into the next great Pentecostal awakening.

A Revival Principle

Now that we have identified how biblical revivals begin, we can easily see the pattern throughout the Bible. The very people of God whose history is traced through the Old Testament began when Abraham met God. Jehovah himself was often identified as the God of Abraham, Isaac, and Jacob—the God who leads through leaders and across generations.

When the Children of Israel were slaves in Egypt, God prepared one man to lead them out of bondage. A whole nation was in trouble, but God revealed himself to Moses in the burning bush. Without a man who talked with God and did what He said there would have been no Exodus, no crossing of the Red Sea, no experience of the Lord's glory on Mount Sinai.

Joshua, who led Israel into the Promised Land, gathered the elders, heads, judges, and officers at Shechem (Joshua 24:1) and dared to declare that the challenge to live for God had to begin with him and his family—"Choose you this day whom ye will serve; . . . but as for me and my house, we will serve the Lord" (verse 15). The people responded, "The Lord our God will we serve, and his voice will we obey" (verse 24). Once the leader made his choice, the people followed.

The Revival under King Josiah

We may see a similar pattern of revival during the reign of King Josiah of Judah, recorded in 2 Kings 22 through 23 and in 2 Chronicles 34 through 35. Since we are looking for biblical patterns of revival, we will consider his story in the light of a greater context and make present applications as we go along.*

It was a time of gross immorality and spiritual neglect in Jerusalem and surrounding Judah, with many of the people turning from Jehovah to heathen gods such as Baal, Asherah, and the "host of heaven" (2 Kings 23:4). Baal was the god of success, prosperity, and good fortune. Asherah was the goddess of fertility, love, and sexuality. The "host of heaven" was a Mesopotamian concept that the sun, moon, and stars were manifestations of gods whose changing patterns affected human events. These pagan gods are still with us and command great followings under the aliases of Prosperity, Sensuality, and Superstition. Much of what is now called the New Age centers on these subjects. If you have any doubt, just watch an evening of television commercials and see if these gods do not dominate all other themes.

Meanwhile in the temple, it was business as usual as the priests performed their duties, in spite of their loss of the Word of God. Nobody had seen a copy of God's Word, as delivered to Moses (2 Chronicles 34:14), for so long that the common people did not even know of its existence. Yet, even without God or His Word, the temple worship continued successfully at a superficial level. Furthermore, the temple coffers were filled with silver, a sure indication that the people liked what was going on there. The temple was no threat to them and made no demands on their lives.

------

*As we have indicated, this distinctively Pentecostal approach of making running applications of Scripture will be no surprise to full-gospel people who have been raised on this style of preaching. By doing so, we do not mean to imply that the original text was written to be applied in this manner but rather that in addition to its explicit truths the Bible contains implied principles by which we may guide our modern lives. King Josiah certainly did not have us in mind when he called for revival in Judah; but, since his revival was a success, we may learn principles from it to offer guidance to our quest for revival today.

Here is a hard fact that we must face: Churches can go on indefinitely with or without the presence of God. Many already have done so! A lot of churches and their ministers fear the supernatural manifestations that occur when God has His way in a church service, and so they continue on dealing with religious symbols rather than yielding to God himself. If every church that displays a cross were truly committed to the cross of Jesus Christ and every congregation that has a descending dove on its church sign were truly filled with the Holy Spirit, we would already have the revival we now seek!

To make matters infinitely worse, the temple shared its once holy grounds with profane altars to Baal (Prosperity), Asherah (Sensuality), and the "host of heaven" (Superstition). The ministers had become so broad-minded that they saw no problem in allowing each person to worship in his own way. The whole program of the temple was oriented toward human response rather than God's response.

One so-called Pentecostal church had on its sign: *For People of All Creeds!* Ecumenicity may have its benefits, but when we allow the world to come inside the church—and inside our lives, since in the New Testament our bodies are the temples of the Holy Ghost (1 Corinthians 6:19)—we desecrate God's holy dwelling place. A great danger in dialogue between religions or church groups is that each may surrender its most objectionable elements in favor of a common compromise. Most often, these influences get into the church through the attitudes and actions of uncommitted Christians who see little difference between one church and another. When our worship can with equal ease be carried out in any kind of church, we have lost our distinctive experience with God and sunk into the vile quicksand of generic religion. The apostle Paul wrote of people "having a form of godliness, but denying the power thereof." He said, "From such turn away" (2 Timothy 3:5).

Furthermore, in spite of its wealth, the temple was in disrepair. The walls were crumbling, and the rafters were giving way. Where there is no love for God there will be no respect for His church. In general, we show what we think about God by how we care for His church—the building, the institution, and the people.

Today, we may have the finest of buildings, a wealth of structure and organization, and a feeling of prosperity because our

59

sanctuaries are filled with contented people and our coffers with tithes and offerings. And yet, if we have neglected God and His Word, the walls of our spiritual church are crumbling around us.

Into this world of trouble came King Josiah, who "did that which was right in the sight of the Lord" (2 Kings 22:2). As with the other revivals, the spiritual awakening of Judah started with the leader. It all began when Josiah noticed the deteriorating condition of the temple. When he learned of all the silver in the temple's storerooms, he sent his personal scribe, Shaphan, to tell Hilkiah, the high priest, to give the money to the workmen to begin the restoration of the house of the Lord. So honest were those carpenters, builders, and masons that "there was no reckoning made with them of the money that was delivered into their hand, because they dealt faithfully" (2 Kings 22:7). The revival began with a renewed interest in the house of God and with sincere and honest people who were willing to work.

But then a marvelous thing happened! In cleaning out the neglected rooms of the temple, they came upon the Book of the Law—which may even have been Moses' original text!* Oh, what changes could come to our churches if we would rediscover God's Word! Today, our ministers preach *about* God, *about* religion, *about* human need . . . but how seldom do they present the living Word, crying out, "Thus saith the Lord!"

The high priest, Hilkiah, gave the scroll to Shaphan, who took it home and read it. How many revivals have started by reading the Word of God! When Shaphan gave his next temple report, he told King Josiah about the discovery and read the scroll to him. At the realization of the horrible neglect and near loss of the Word of God, Josiah rent his clothes and called for Hilkiah and his priests to seek God on the nation's behalf. They did not know how, for speaking directly with God had never been a part of their ministerial functions; so they went to a godly woman named Huldah the prophetess, who consulted with God, learned of His wrath, and delivered His message to King Josiah and the

---

*Some think that Hilkiah found the entire Pentateuch, the first five books of the Bible. This seems unlikely when we see that it was read in one sitting. Others believe it was either the Book of Deuteronomy or the portion of that book in which Moses and the people renewed the covenant in the plains of Moab (Deuteronomy 28 through 31).

people of Judah. Even in the worst of times, there are godly people who know how to talk with God. It is certain that there can be no revival without effective prayer. James 5:16 says, "Confess your faults one to another, and pray one for another, that ye may be healed. The effectual fervent prayer of a righteous man availeth much."

Through the prophetess Huldah, God said to King Josiah, "Because thine heart was tender, and thou hast humbled thyself before the Lord, . . . and hast rent thy clothes, and wept before me; I also have heard thee, saith the Lord" (2 Kings 22:19). This was the secret of Josiah's revival. It was not enough to discover the Word of God in the temple; it had to come to new life in his own heart, which was tender toward God. He humbled himself before the Lord, tore his royal garments as a sign of repentance and grief, and wept before the Lord. (So much for unemotional religion!) When Josiah took that attitude and those actions, God heard him.

Josiah called together all the people of Judah, small and great, priests and prophets, and read to them "all the words of the book of the covenant which was found in the house of the Lord" (2 Kings 23:2). The king stood by a pillar of the temple and made a covenant before the Lord "to walk after the Lord, and to keep his commandments and his testimonies and his statutes with all [his] heart and all [his] soul, to perform the words of this covenant that were written in this book" (23:3). And all the people stood to their feet in agreement with the covenant.

This is what needs to happen in every church—to repent, to pray, and to lead the people to a new covenant with God. Revival comes in no other way! Today's equivalent of standing by the pillar is our kneeling at the altar. If every person in our churches would kneel at an altar today and make that same covenant, the revival would begin.

There is no need to go into detail about all the effects of the revival in Judah. The results began when the high priest, Hilkiah; the priests of the second order; and the keepers of the door carried out of the temple all the paraphernalia of the heathen gods, burned them, and dumped their ashes outside the border of Judah. That's how our revival will start, too—when our pastors, staff members, and ushers purge the church of its ungodliness! Catch some of Jesus' holy anger as He upset the moneychangers' tables, released the captive doves, and cried out, "It is written, My house shall be called the house of prayer; but ye have made it a den of thieves" (Matthew 21:13). If we want God to move in, we first must move some things out!

Josiah cleaned up all the land, destroyed the heathen altars, and rid the country of its idolatry. What would happen in America if our national leaders would follow his example?

Ezra's Revival

Another Old Testament revival is recorded in chapters 9 and 10 of Ezra. This one is less understood because of its implications for a holy separation of the people of God. The demands of holiness have never been popular except in periods of revival; indeed, a common rejection of standards of righteousness may be at the core of the problem when a spirit of revival is lacking.

In spite of King Josiah's revival, after his death the people of Judah returned to their sins. In every revival there will be those who are truly repentant and revived, but there will be others, perhaps the majority, who will be caught up in the spirit of the revival but without personal repentance. Such people revert to their former ways as soon as the enthusiasm of the revival is over or the leaders change. Then, having greater guilt for their rejection of God's mercy, they continue on in worse condition than they were before. Something evil happens on the downside of a diminishing revival. With the return of heathen immorality came the condemnation of the prophesied wrath of a spurned and neglected God.

As the judgment of God, the Babylonians conquered Judah, destroyed Jerusalem and the temple, and carried the people into slavery in Babylon. We usually hear that the Babylonian captivity lasted seventy years, but for most of the people it never ended. Only a remnant, a tithe of about ten percent, ever returned to Jerusalem. The rest were scattered even further.

Babylon fell to the Medes and Persians, and it was under the Persians that some of the Jews were allowed to return to their homeland to rebuild the temple and the walls of Jerusalem. The Book of Ezra tells of this return under the leadership of Zerubbabel. Yet, much like modern Israel, they returned to the land without returning to God. Having lived in a heathen land, the Jews brought some of its idolatry back with them. Many of the men, even the leaders, married "strange wives" from among the ungodly peoples who had moved into Palestine during the Babylonian captivity. Worse, they were "doing according to their abominations" (Ezra 9:1).

Ezra, "a ready scribe in the law of Moses" (7:6), had "prepared his heart to seek the law of the Lord, and to do it, and to teach in Israel statutes and judgments" (7:10). When he and others of a second migration arrived in Jerusalem, they were horrified at the spiritual condition of the first migration. Some of the princes reported, "The people of Israel, and the priests, and the Levites, have not separated themselves from the people of the lands, doing according to their abominations, even of the Canaanites, the Hittites, the Perizzites, the Jebusites, the Ammonites, the Moabites, the Egyptians, and the Amorites" (9:1). We may still have those *parasites* with us!

The lack of separation from the world is still the most serious problem among us. The apostle John wrote, "Love not the world, neither the things that are in the world. If any man love the world, the love of the Father is not in him" (1 John 2:15). After asking, "What fellowship hath righteousness with unrighteousness? and what communion hath light with darkness?" (2 Corinthians 6:14), the apostle Paul picked up Isaiah's exhortation, declaring, "Wherefore come out from among them, and be ye separate, saith the Lord, and touch not the unclean thing; and I will receive you" (verse 17). Separation from sin is required for revival.

When Ezra heard the report, he rent his garments, plucked his head and beard, and sat in the rebuilt temple appalled. Others who felt as he did joined him as he sat stunned until the evening sacrifice. He then rose up from his self-abasement, fell on his knees with his hands spread out to the Lord, and prayed a prayer of repentance to God, saying, "O my God, I am ashamed and blush to lift up my face to thee, my God: for our iniquities are increased over our head, and our trespass is grown up unto the heavens" (Ezra 9:6).

Included in his prayer, Ezra said, "And now for a little space grace hath been showed from the Lord our God, to leave us a remnant to escape, and to give us a nail in his holy place, that our God may lighten our eyes, and give us a little reviving in our bondage" (verse 8). God in His grace had taken mercy on His people and had allowed a remnant to escape from the captivity. In reviving them, God gave them three things.

First, He gave them "a nail in his holy place." The idea is that of a stake to which one might tether an animal. The people of God are to be tethered to a stake in the house of God, limited in how far they may stray from their center in Him. Second, He gave them a new light in their eyes. Just look at the difference in the faces of revived and unrevived Christians and you will see what Ezra meant. You need only walk into a church to know if it is revived. Third, God gave them "a little reviving." This was before the people's repentance. A little revival is not enough; we have had sparkles of revival here and there in our darkness, but now we need a greater move of God to light up the whole church.

"Now when Ezra had prayed, and when he had confessed, weeping and casting himself down before the house of God, there assembled unto him out of Israel a very great congregation of men and women and children: for the people wept very sore" (Ezra 10:1). When the leader repented, the people followed.

Through their spokesman, Shechaniah, the people said, "We have trespassed against our God, and have taken strange wives of the people of the land: yet now there is hope in Israel concerning this thing. Now therefore let us make a covenant with our God" (10:2–3). Shechaniah said to Ezra, "Arise; for this matter belongeth unto thee: we also will be with thee: be of good courage, and do it" (verse 4). Ezra rose up in the authority of the Lord and went into a time of fasting and prayer before he dealt with the problem.

It was winter, and cold rain was coming down in Jerusalem as Ezra gathered the people again in the open court of the temple. He said, "Ye have transgressed, and have taken strange wives, to increase the trespass of Israel. Now therefore make confession unto the Lord God of your fathers, and do his pleasure: and separate yourselves from the people of the land, and from the strange wives" (verses 10–11). The congregation answered with a loud voice, "As thou hast said, so must we do" (verse 12). Over the following days, those who repented separated themselves as promised and purified themselves with sacrifices. Those who did not repent had their lands confiscated and were excommunicated from the people (10:8).

With Judaism revived, the stage was being prepared for the coming of the Messiah, born in Bethlehem of Judea of the family line of King David. Ezra's revival was a vital link in the chain of events that would bring Christ to the world.

In an article titled "What Revival Means," James K. Bridges, then superintendent of the North Texas District and now our general treasurer, wrote, "The Assemblies of God was born in the fires of revival—a revival brought about by prayer, fasting, witnessing, living in the power of the Holy Spirit, and obeying the Word of God."

In every case, a revival occurs when the people of God follow a Spirit-anointed leader and return to their covenant with God. The same things that brought revival in the days of Josiah and Ezra produced the Pentecostal revival; and the same will be required for the great awakening to come.

6

A Rediscovery of Pentecost

For thousands of years it had been a mystery how the ancient Egyptians made papyrus. People knew they laid moistened pieces of the pith of sedge Cyperus papyrus over one another and pressed or pounded them into the Western world's earliest paper, but no one had been able to duplicate the process. Recently, Egyptians rediscovered the procedure and now are making papyrus nearly indistinguishable from the ancient specimens that have been preserved. When they returned to the original method, they obtained original results.

Something similar happened with original Christianity. Bible readers knew that it once existed and was very different from that of their own churches, and yet nobody knew how to duplicate it. At the turn of the twentieth century, spiritually hungry, Bible-informed people rediscovered the baptism in the Holy Spirit, which was the key ingredient in the revival of authentic Christianity. And when they returned to the original methods, they obtained original results.

Think about this: At the writing of this book, it has been eighty years since our fathers organized the Assemblies of God at Hot Springs, Arkansas. It has been ninety-three years since the beginning of the Pentecostal movement at Topeka (in what they called "nineteen aught one"). We still have a few people who were babies or little children when our founding events occurred, but we have no one left who remembers. Someone born at the turn of this century would have had children born in

66

the twenties and thirties. Those children would have had children in the forties and fifties, who were to bear children in the sixties and seventies. These latter are now our younger ministers. Their children, born in the eighties and nineties, are beginning to produce the next generation of preachers for the twenty-first century . . . for the new millennium.

Few family albums ever show more than four generations in one picture. We might see children, parents, grandparents, and great-grandparents; but the picture seldom includes great-great-grandparents. We don't remember our earliest childhood and may have some memory problems in our old age, so people who live past ninety may have an effective memory span of about eighty years. Perhaps this is why most church denominations lose sight of their original purpose after about eighty years. It's the limit of our memory span.

Many of us believe the Assemblies of God can break that pattern. In spite of our present signs of aging, we believe we have found the fountain of youth. The Pentecostal movement has rediscovered the original formula of the Day of Pentecost. In a significant sense we are quite different from other historical churches. We have a strong belief in the manual, the New Testament, that will be passed down to future generations. We may be running out of memory, but God has not forgotten. This is not a movement of the early twentieth century; it is a revival of the Early Church, the church of the living God of Abraham, Isaac, and Jacob—the One who continues His work through the generations.

However, if we are to have a fresh revival of original, New Testament, apostolic, Pentecostal Christianity, we must search the Scriptures and find out exactly what needs to be revived.

Oh, What a Day!

The Day of Pentecost in A.D. 30 changed the world, for it was the birth of the Church. On that day, thousands of devoted Jews from all over the Roman Empire had gathered in Jerusalem to celebrate the giving of the Law. In even more ancient times, it had been an agricultural feast related to the harvest season. By the first century A.D., however, its meaning had changed. If we could have asked Peter, James, or John why so many people had gathered in the temple, they would have told us it was to celebrate the giving of the Law on Mount Sinai. (See Exodus 34:22; Leviticus 23:17–20; Deuteronomy 16:9–10.)

Exodus 19:18–19 says, "And mount Sinai was altogether on a smoke, because the Lord descended upon it in fire: and the smoke thereof ascended as the smoke of a furnace, and the whole mount quaked greatly. And when the voice of the trumpet sounded long, and waxed louder and louder, Moses spake, and God answered him by a voice."

Now that we know what they were celebrating, we may imagine the temple scene at nine o'clock that morning when crowds of people were milling about the open courtyard.* It had been only seven weeks since Jesus of Nazareth, who many believed was the Christ, the promised Messiah, was crucified, and rumors were going through the multitudes that He indeed was the Christ and may even have risen from the dead. The apostle Paul said that more than five hundred people had seen Jesus alive after His death and resurrection (1 Corinthians 15:6).

Just then, there was a commotion in an area called Solomon's Porch. Luke described it this way in Acts 2:1–4: "And when the day of Pentecost was fully come, they were all with one accord in one place. And suddenly there came a sound from heaven as of a rushing mighty wind, and it filled all the house where they were sitting. And there appeared unto them cloven tongues like as of fire, and it sat upon each of them. And they were all filled with the Holy Ghost, and began to speak with other tongues, as the Spirit gave them utterance."

Like the fire and smoke on Mount Sinai witnessed by the Children of Israel when God gave the Law, the 120 witnessed a sound like "a rushing mighty wind" and "cloven tongues like as

---

*During the ten days between Christ's ascension and the outpouring of the Holy Spirit at Pentecost, the apostles were residing in the Upper Room. Acts 1:13–14 lists those who were there. However, the upstairs room of a Jewish house could not have held 120 people, far less the thousands who were converted that day. Luke said, "And they worshipped him, and returned to Jerusalem with great joy: and were continually in the temple, praising and blessing God" (Luke 24:52–53). Therefore, the prayer and supplication that began in the Upper Room had moved to the temple, where the outpouring of the Holy Spirit occurred. Acts 3:11 and 5:12 place the first believers in the temple area called Solomon's Porch.

of fire." Yet, true to God's instructions to Moses that it was to be a harvest-related festival the Day of Pentecost marked the beginning of the Christian harvest of souls when three thousand people were converted to Jesus Christ. At the outpouring of divine power at Mount Sinai, "Moses spake, and God answered him by a voice," and on the Day of Pentecost the Spirit of God entered into the 120, and they "spake with other tongues, as the Spirit gave them utterance."

To the degree that Israel strayed from God's commandments, to that extent they failed and angered God. Any departure from the Law was a deterioration of the religion and grounds for a loss of God's favor. The same must be said of original Christianity. There is only one true Church, founded by Jesus Christ and taught by His first followers. Any departure from original Christianity is a deterioration of the faith and a direct cause of a loss of God's blessing.

Preparation for Pentecost

The early Pentecostal movement discovered that when we go back to New Testament Christianity we get New Testament results. Those who awoke spiritually to this truth were filled with the Holy Spirit and spoke in other tongues, just like the first Christians. There was a renewed understanding of the death and resurrection of Jesus Christ and an acute awareness of His promised second coming. Sinners were being saved and added daily to the church. People were healed, delivered, and miraculously protected. Praise was enthusiastic and out loud, and something supernatural was expected in every service.

The question is, How may we revive that kind of Christianity today? And that raises other questions.

First, are we really willing to let go of our traditions and tight control and allow the Holy Spirit to manifest himself in miraculous and surprising ways? Second, are we really willing to fall on our faces before God and repent of our sins? Third, are we really willing to allow our people to respond to the Holy Spirit spontaneously and without ecclesiastical or social restrictions? That is, in how many of our churches will shouts of praise be considered a problem? Fourth, are we really willing to pray—to repent, to fast and pray, to go into prayer and supplication, to intercede?

Some of the people in the Upper Room (Acts 1:13) had been with Jesus throughout His ministry. They had heard His teachings and seen His miracles. Years later, John wrote, "That which was from the beginning, which we have heard, which we have seen with our eyes, which we have looked upon, and our hands have handled, of the Word of life; . . . that which we have seen and heard declare we unto you, that ye also may have fellowship with us: and truly our fellowship is with the Father, and with his Son Jesus Christ" (1 John 1:1–3). John clearly offers the experience of the first Christians as the model for our fellowship today.

Those first followers personally witnessed Jesus' death and resurrection. The cross and the empty tomb had absolutely changed their lives. Then, after receiving the Great Commission to spread the gospel over the earth, they saw the Lord's ascension and received the word of the angels, who said, "This same Jesus, which is taken up from you into heaven, shall so come in like manner as ye have seen him go into heaven" (Acts 1:11). Those experiences with Jesus Christ were fresh on their minds as they joined together in one accord in prayer and supplication. Prayer is conversing with God in words, and supplication is pouring out our hearts to God with the emotions. Faith and feelings are inseparable elements of the Christian life, like the two sides of a coin. The willingness to enter into passionate prayer was a necessary prerequisite to the Pentecostal experience.

For us to have a Pentecostal revival, we must experience the same preparation as the apostles: (1) be personally acquainted with Jesus Christ, having taken full note of His example and teachings in the Gospels, (2) experience the shame and agony of the cross, (3) witness His resurrection power, (4) realize that He has ascended into heaven, where He intercedes for us before the throne of God, (5) be committed to the fellowship of the church in unity, (6) join with others in prolonged prayer and supplication, and (7) accept supernatural phenomena when they occur.

Many people talk about revival, but when it actually comes they are afraid to enter into it. We have become so trained at standing on the sidelines as curious bystanders that we are not prepared for the vulnerability of personal involvement. We are observers rather than obtainers, spectators rather than participants. The decision to enter into worship instead of merely watching others being blessed is a major threshold to cross as we seek personal and corporate revival.

Having said that, let us make it clear that what we are seeking is not some intense emotional state, although there never has been a revival without it. We are not seeking a condition but Christ himself. The condition will follow the encounter. Revival is a living relationship in fellowship with Christ and His church and in witness to the world.

Pentecostal Characteristics

The phrase "one accord" appears five times in the first five chapters of the Book of Acts, thus emphasizing its great importance for any church's spiritual awakening.

Glen D. Cole, pastor of Capital Christian Center in Sacramento, California, and an executive presbyter of the Assemblies of God, said,

> One of the great statements on revival in Acts 2 is this —"They were all with one accord." The apostle Paul pleaded with the Corinthian believers to "speak the same thing, and that there be no divisions among you; but that ye be perfectly joined together in the same mind and in the same judgment [discernment]" (1 Corinthians 1:10). The strength of Christianity is in unity! First Corinthians 12 shows us clearly that there are "many members, yet but one body" (12:20).

The first group activity of the Early Church was prolonged prayer and supplication. The first condition of the church was unity, being in one accord. The first spiritual experience of the church was the baptism in the Holy Spirit. The first spiritual response of the church was that they all spoke in other tongues—that is, in languages they had never learned. There were many witnesses present who confirmed that the sounds they were making were in real languages—"And how hear we every man in our own tongue, wherein we were born?" (Acts 2:8). So powerful was the experience and so "lost in the Spirit" were the believers that the onlookers thought they were drunk. This may give us some indication of what to expect in a truly Spirit-filled church!

The experience of speaking in other tongues is in every case a miracle. It is an indisputable proof because it is utterly impossi-

71

ble to make any sense in a language we have not learned. Yet, there have been many, many incidents over this century when people who spoke foreign languages have testified that someone speaking in other tongues was communicating clearly in their language. In the evidence of speaking in other tongues the Lord gave us a proof that cannot be duplicated or denied.

Those first Christians were all filled with the Holy Spirit and spoke in other tongues "the wonderful works of God" (Acts 2:11). Yet, when they looked up and saw the multitude of unsaved people, they stopped speaking in tongues and preached the gospel with power and authority in the common language. This characteristic of turning spiritual experience into successful evangelism is at the heart of what it means to be Pentecostal. Peter gave an altar call, and three thousand people were saved. Pentecostal preaching always anticipates some kind of immediate response from the hearers as well as long-term results. After being baptized in water, the new converts received the same baptism in the Holy Spirit as the first group had experienced earlier in the day (Acts 2:38).

Something supernatural happened whenever the New Testament Christians had church. It might have been a healing, a deliverance, or some miracle. It might have been a Spirit-anointed sermon. And, there is no greater miracle than the salvation of a soul with the transformation from sinner to saint. This is a key factor missing in many churches today, for we have replaced the active power of God with abstract symbols. We have meetings *about* Jesus Christ rather than *with* Him! He said, "For where two or three are gathered together in my name, there am I in the midst of them" (Matthew 18:20). If that is true, then we should expect something supernatural to happen in every service!

We could go through the Book of Acts to show case after case of supernatural phenomena—healings, miraculous protection, casting out devils, and much more. Such signs and wonders are a normal result of the spiritual environment of a Pentecostal church. They happen in the context of two elements working together: expectation of the supernatural and all-out evangelism. We sometimes wonder why good Christians suffer and are not healed. A close study of the New Testament will reveal a strong connection between preaching the gospel and seeing miracles, between evangelism and the supernatural. We have heard it said that miracles happen along the cutting edge of evangelism. Divine healing was not given to replace good sense or medical care but as a sign to support the preaching of the gospel.

After telling His disciples to go and preach the gospel, Jesus promised, "These signs shall follow them that believe": casting out devils, speaking in tongues, receiving miraculous protection, and healing the sick (Mark 16:17–18). In response, the first Christians "went forth, and preached every where, the Lord working with them, and confirming the word with signs following" (Mark 16:20). Soul winning is the context in which miracles occur. Add to that the anticipation and expectation of the supernatural that comes with revival, and miracles are bound to happen. Faith is necessary, yes, but it is easier to believe for the impossible in the rarefied atmosphere of a Pentecostal revival.

The Initial Physical Evidence

Before going on, we must reply to a present trend among some scholars to claim that the Book of Acts cannot be used as a basis for doctrine because it is a narrative. First, they are wrong biblically because "all scripture is given by inspiration of God, and is profitable for doctrine, for reproof, for correction, for instruction in righteousness: that the man of God may be perfect, thoroughly furnished unto all good works" (2 Timothy 3:16–17). Yes, the apostle Paul was writing of what we call the Old Testament, but a basic claim of the Christian faith is that the New Testament is part of the canon of Scripture and to be accepted as the Word of God.

The second reason they are wrong is that most of the Bible is narrative and included in "all scripture." The fact that the Book of Acts is historical only adds to its credibility. The Gospels also are narratives. Are we not to base doctrine on the words and deeds of Jesus?

The third reason these critics are wrong is that their manner of thinking would eventually remove the whole Bible from doctrinal use. If we were to accept their judgment that the narrative books are not doctrinal, they might then say we cannot use the Psalms because they are poetry, the Prophets because they are prophecy, the Epistles because they are private letters, or the Book of Revelation because it is apocalyptic.

What they are attempting to do is to remove our evidence for speaking in tongues as the initial physical evidence of the baptism in the Holy Spirit. Let us make our Pentecostal position distinct and intelligible for all to understand with the following logic. The New Testament church is the model for the church in any age; the first thing the first believers did when they "were all filled with the Holy Ghost" was that they "began to speak with other tongues, as the Spirit gave them utterance" (Acts 2:4); therefore, the first thing we will do when we are filled with the Holy Spirit is to speak in other tongues.

We call speaking in tongues the initial physical evidence of the baptism in the Holy Spirit because it was the first thing that happened when they received the experience. It was physical in the sense that it was something definite that they did. Some people argue this point, but to do so they have to insert something else between "they were all filled with the Holy Ghost" and "[they] began to speak with other tongues, as the Spirit gave them utterance." Acts 2:4 leaves no room for such insertions. Of course there are other evidences of the Holy Spirit baptism, but they do not precede speaking in other tongues. We do not deny other spiritual events in people's lives, but they should not call their subjective experiences the baptism in the Holy Spirit when such experiences do not align with Acts 2:4. It is the original standard, and there must be no compromise.

Jesus faced two main sects of Judaism, the Pharisees and the Sadducees. The Pharisees were the legalists who held everyone to the letter of the Law and added their own burden of rules; the Sadducees were the liberals who did not believe in such doctrines as the resurrection, life after death, or the existence of angels. We still face the legalists and the liberals and must not allow either to destroy our faith. Yes, we can use the Book of Acts as a source for our doctrine and will continue to do so.

The Gifts of the Spirit

In 1 Corinthians 12:1–10, the apostle Paul gave us a list of the nine gifts of the Spirit. After saying that we need to know about such things, he said that these supernatural occurrences are not caused by different spirits, as the heathen believe, but are all from the one Holy Spirit. They are not resident in individuals, but are manifested through them as the Holy Spirit requires and inspires. It is not proper to say, "I have the gift of healing." Rather, the whole Church has the gifts of healing from

74

the Spirit himself, who manifests himself through those whose faith allows Him to operate. Nevertheless, we must recognize that once a person has been used of the Spirit to manifest a particular gift, it is much easier for that believer to minister in a similar manner again and again. Yet, every Christian should potentially be available to the Holy Spirit for whichever gifts are needed.

Paul said, "But the manifestation of the Spirit is given to every man to profit withal" (1 Corinthians 12:7). That is, the gifts may be manifested through individuals, but they are intended for the profit of the whole Church. First Corinthians 14 makes it clear that these gifts operate mostly in church services. In enumerating the spiritual gifts, Paul wrote in 1 Corinthians 12:8–10, "For to one is given by the Spirit the word of wisdom; to another the word of knowledge by the same Spirit; to another faith by the same Spirit; to another the gifts of healing by the same Spirit; to another the working of miracles; to another prophecy; to another discerning of spirits; to another divers kinds of tongues; to another the interpretation of tongues."

We need only read that list to see that any one of these spiritual phenomena could cause consternation in many churches today. People talk about Almighty God, but when He does anything even the slightest bit mighty they go into shock and considerable fear. A truly Pentecostal church not only will believe in such occurrences but also will teach its people to yield to the Holy Spirit and believe God for one or more of the gifts in every service.

We may think of the nine gifts of the Spirit in three categories of three gifts each—those of knowing, those of doing, and those of speaking.

GIFTS OF KNOWING	Word of Wisdom
	Word of Knowledge
	Discerning of Spirits
GIFTS OF DOING	Faith
	Gifts of Healing
	Working of Miracles
GIFTS OF SPEAKING	Prophecy
	Speaking in Tongues
	Interpretation of Tongues

The word of wisdom is listed first because it is required for the operation of any of the other gifts. For example, a person may be inspired to utter a prophecy, but divine wisdom will be required to know when to speak. Among other things, it is the gift of timing for the others. When we find ourselves operating in the Spirit and realize that events are being coordinated outside our own minds, that is the gift of wisdom at work, usually in conjunction with other gifts.

The word of knowledge is miraculous knowing without prior learning. That is, the Holy Spirit reveals information to the believer, particularly in times of high spiritual activity such as prayer or preaching. It is not to be misused, as often happens today, by telling someone, "I have a word from the Lord for you." One of the differences between Old Testament and New Testament religion is that in the New we no longer have to go through a priest or prophet to get the word of the Lord but have direct access to the throne of God. The Holy Spirit works in many ways and may use other people to confirm the Father's will for us, but He will always speak to us personally. Indeed, that is a major purpose of the baptism in the Holy Spirit.

Both of these gifts of knowing are called a "word" because they are manifested in specific incidents. The person through whom they operate may not always be wise or knowledgeable. None of the gifts imply a continuing state but operate for particular times and occasions.

The gift of discerning of spirits, often called the gift of discernment, is intended to tell the believer what is happening in the spirit world. It is difficult to distinguish between this gift and that of a word of knowledge, although in general we may consider knowledge as revelation of facts and discernment as perception of what is going on spiritually. It may be that knowledge operates in the physical and mental world, and discernment relates to spiritual activity. It certainly is not a gift of suspicion to be used as any excuse for gossip, slander, or show of spiritual superiority. To the contrary, it must be manifested with the utmost of humility and compassion.

The doing gifts of faith, healing, and working of miracles also overlap and in many cases operate in combination. There are moments when the Holy Spirit gives to a Spirit-filled believer an added measure of faith to accomplish His will. Gifts of healing are plural because God works in many ways to heal—

instantaneously, progressively, or by directing us to effective medical treatment. Yet, we will experience more immediate healings as revival grows. The working of miracles differs from healing only in the effects. A healing *is* a miracle. Literally, Paul called this gift "the operation of works of power." This covers a wide range of what happens in a Pentecostal church service.

The speaking gifts are best known because they are spoken forth and are obvious to any hearers, while some of the other gifts may not come to the attention of some people present. Prophecy is speaking forth under the direct inspiration of the Holy Spirit. A person might speak out a prophecy in a church service. Here again the timing from the word of wisdom must be manifested. Most often, the gift of prophecy operates through anointed preaching. Many excellent sermons are the Bible-based expression of a well-prepared minister; there is also an anointed state when a Pentecostal preacher focuses on a subject of immediate concern to, or need of, the congregation that would be impossible for other kinds of preaching.

The gifts of "divers kinds of tongues" and interpretation of tongues always must work together. The gift of speaking in tongues is the miracle of making utterances in a language the speaker has not learned. People may imitate it by making odd sounds, but whenever it is real language it is a miracle that cannot be counterfeited. The gift of varieties of tongues listed here differs from the speaking in tongues for all believers in that this is for the whole church and is to be interpreted as a message from the Lord. As with prophecy, it must be accompanied by the wisdom of proper timing. The gift of interpretation of tongues may operate through the same individual, but it often is more credible if someone else interprets. Some Christians have the idea that prophecy and the combination of tongues and interpretation are synonymous or accomplish the same purpose. This may sometimes be true, but whereas tongues and interpretation are easily identified as such, prophecy often occurs without the hearers realizing it. The Lord uses Spirit-filled people to say what He wants said, and the hearer might not recognize the source.

We have gone into some detail on the gifts of the Spirit because the operation of these spiritual manifestations and utterances will be extremely important in the coming revival.

As the new awakening occurs, there will be an increase in spiritual phenomena in church services; and the pastor who truly wants revival must become spiritually alert and learn to operate in the Spirit himself rather than seeing these things as unwanted interruptions in his own control of the service. The revived and spiritually aware minister will know when and how God is moving. When both the pastor and the people are in the Spirit, we may understand Paul's admonition about this very subject: "Let all things be done decently and in order" (1 Corinthians 14:40).

The Fruit of the Spirit

There has been some confusion in the Pentecostal movement about the fruit of the Spirit in Galatians 5:22–23, "But the fruit of the Spirit is love, joy, peace, long-suffering, gentleness, goodness, faith, meekness, temperance." The source of this puzzlement has been that, since these are "of the Spirit," they must come about because of the baptism in the Holy Spirit. This is a mistake because the very next verse says, "And they that are Christ's have crucified the flesh with the affections and lusts" (verse 24). That is, these are the characteristics of those who have been saved through Christ and are living consistently holy lives.

The gifts of the Spirit are manifested whole and for specific occasions, but the fruit of the Spirit begins with the right seed and grows into Christian maturity. We must remember, of course, that in the New Testament all born-again believers were also baptized in the Holy Spirit. If we were in a true state of revival, we would have no need of pointing out this distinction.

There is one similarity between the lists of the nine gifts of the Spirit and the nine fruit of the Spirit. As the first gift of the Spirit is wisdom because it is needed for the operation of all the other gifts, so the first in the list of the fruit of the Spirit is love. It, too, is required for the development of all the other Christian qualities.

There also is a great difference between the two lists. Whereas the separate gifts may operate through different individuals, every Christian is expected to grow all the fruit of the Spirit.

When the Holy Spirit has His way, we will not have to produce the fruit of the Spirit by our efforts or plead with people to allow the Spirit to use them in the spiritual gifts. The gifts and fruit of the Spirit will come spontaneously in a revived Pentecostal church. We will regain our Pentecostal experience the same way the Early Church received theirs—by experience with Christ, prayer and supplication, and being in one accord in the house of the Lord.

7

What It Means to Be Pentecostal

Throughout our churches today there is general agreement that we are not as committed to being Pentecostal as we used to be. We may not fully understand what fired the souls of our Pentecostal forefathers, but we do know we have lost something that we must regain if we are to fulfill our divine purpose.

It is time to call our people back to God, to seek for a new Pentecostal revival, and to insist that true religion is New Testament Christianity as taught by Jesus Christ and passed down to us by the apostles.

The Cost of Pentecost

On the Day of Pentecost, the people who observed the first outpouring of the Holy Spirit asked, "What meaneth this?" Peter answered, "This is that which was spoken by the prophet Joel," and proceeded to quote Joel 2:28–32 that God would pour out His Spirit on all flesh, regardless of gender, age, or social position. He would accompany that outpouring with signs and wonders and use His people to proclaim salvation to the whole world.

The Pentecostal church was never supposed to be a branch of Christianity but the very trunk of the tree. It was for *all* flesh, *all* your sons and daughters, *all* your young and old people, *all* your servants and handmaidens. It was for *all* the "whosoever" who would call on the name of the Lord and be saved! Every Christian and each church is supposed to be Pentecostal.

We are losing our sense of certainty. Today we are too understanding, too open-minded, too compromising. Our Pentecostal forefathers called themselves "full gospel," because anything less than the whole truth was no truth at all. They honestly believed that any church that was not Pentecostal in belief and behavior was wrong.

At the end of the first Christian sermon, Peter said, "Repent, and be baptized every one of you [everybody] in the name of Jesus Christ for the remission of sins [everybody], and ye shall receive the gift of the Holy Ghost [everybody]. For the promise is unto you [the first generation], and to your children [the next generation], and to all that are afar off [generation after generation], even as many as the Lord our God shall call [all generations]" (Acts 2:38–39).

There is a cost to Pentecost—a total commitment to Jesus Christ and His Word. Anything less than the whole heart, whole soul, whole mind, and whole strength is an abomination and a stench in the nostrils of a holy God.

How to Be Pentecostal

Let us define what it means to be Pentecostal. Our definition must be as clear as the crystal sea before the throne of God and yet so simple that anyone anywhere at any time may understand and follow it. Here is our basic definition of Pentecostal Christians: Pentecostal Christians are those believers in Jesus Christ and His gospel who identify themselves in belief, experience, practice, and priority with the original Church born on the Day of Pentecost and described in the New Testament.

It's as simple as that: Pentecostal Christianity is true Christianity. In the New Testament we find our beliefs, religious experiences, practices, and priorities. The Bible is our manual, and the original Church our model.

The Pentecostal Paradigm

A paradigm is an outstandingly clear or typical example or archetype. That is exactly what the original Church is for us. That first model may be adapted to different cultures and social orders, but its beliefs, experiences, practices, and priorities remain constant.

For example, all people who are filled with the Holy Spirit

will "speak with other tongues, as the Spirit [gives] them utterance" (Acts 2:4). Speaking in tongues is not the only sign of the baptism in the Holy Spirit, but it is the initial physical evidence that the experience has occurred. This experience will be the same everywhere; such variables as clothing styles, native languages, or whether the people are standing, sitting, or prostrate on the floor may differ greatly. Adaptability to language and culture also was a characteristic of the Early Church.

This leads us to the question: What are the core concepts that will not change?

Pentecostal Beliefs

This is not the time to go into a full description of original, New Testament, apostolic doctrine. Suffice it to say that the Early Church "continued steadfastly in the apostles' doctrine and fellowship, and in breaking of bread, and in prayers" (Acts 2:42). What began on the Day of Pentecost was supposed to continue throughout the Church Age.

We are not a credal church in the sense of repeating the Christian creeds as acts of worship, but the original doctrines of the Church are vital to us. The Apostles' Creed was not written by the apostles themselves but by second-century Christians who wanted to preserve the original doctrines of Jesus' first followers. Here is a translation from the Greek text:[*]

> I believe in God the Father Almighty, Creator of heaven and earth, and in Jesus Christ His only Son, our Lord, who was conceived by the Holy Spirit, born of the Virgin Mary, suffered under Pontius Pilate, was crucified, died, and was buried. He descended into hell and the third day rose again from the dead; He ascended into heaven and sits at the right hand of God the Father Almighty, from where He will come to judge the living and the dead. I believe in the Holy Spirit, the Holy Universal Church, the fellowship of saints, the forgiveness of sins, the resurrection of the body, and life everlasting. Amen.

Of course, we understand that "Holy Universal Church" refers to the whole Church always and everywhere. The "fellowship of saints" was a later addition to the Apostles' Creed, but we can accept it if it means the fellowship of all Christian believers of

---

*Translation from the Greek by David A. Womack.

all times—living, dead, and yet to be born—who will make up the saints of God in heaven.

These were the core beliefs of the Early Church, which they learned from the apostles. They are still the doctrines of all true Christians everywhere. When we say we believe in the Holy Spirit, we mean all that that term implies from the New Testament, including the Spirit's work of bringing us to Christ, convicting us of sin, leading us in the Word, filling us with His holy presence, giving us the utterance of tongues, empowering us for Christian witness, ministering through the spiritual gifts, and guiding us to the very gates of heaven.

Apostolic doctrine centered on the life, death, resurrection, and promised return of Jesus Christ. This core of doctrine was called the *euaggélion*—the *"gospel,"* "evangel," or "good news." Another broader area of apostolic doctrine was the *kērugma*— the *"preaching"* of the apostles. The third source of doctrine was the New Testament *writings* of the apostles and other first-century Christians. And the fourth source was the Old Testament *Scriptures,* which they accepted as inspired by God. We find all four of these sources in the Bible, our infallible rule of faith and conduct. The apostle Paul wrote to the Galatians, "But though we, or an angel from heaven, preach any other gospel unto you than that which we have preached unto you, let him be accursed" (1:8).

Pentecostal Experience

Many Pentecostals speak of four cardinal doctrines: salvation, the baptism in the Holy Spirit, divine healing, and the second coming of Christ. Actually, these are four cardinal experiences, for they are spiritual events based on doctrine. Belief must precede experience. They do not deal with other essential theology such as the nature of God or the inerrancy of the Bible. They do not even include such experiences as water baptism, Communion, answered prayer, spiritual guidance, signs and wonders, or casting out devils—all of which were vital to the Early Church.

Pentecostal people have always been experience-oriented. At Pentecost, the apostle Peter said, "Repent, and be baptized every one of you . . . for the remission of sins, and ye shall receive the gift of the Holy Ghost" (Acts 2:38)—all experiences. People are not saved merely by joining a church and accepting its doctrinal statement but by a critical moment of repentance of sin and acceptance of Jesus Christ as Savior and Lord. Salvation is a definite experience that occurs at a particular time and place and is followed by the separate experiences of water baptism and the baptism in the Holy Spirit.

There was a clear connection between Passover and Pentecost. The Day of Pentecost occurred fifty days after Passover and was a celebration of the giving of the Law on Mount Sinai (the opening of the harvest season in more ancient times). The word "Pentecost" was from the Greek *pente* ("five") plus *ēkonta* (the decimal designation), hence the Greek word for "fifty." As God sent down fire from heaven and thunderings on the holy mountain when He gave His law, so He sent the sound of a mighty wind and tongues of fire on the temple mount when He poured out His Holy Spirit.

On the Day of Pentecost, they were *all* filled with the Holy Ghost and spoke with other tongues (Acts 2:4), so we believe that God intends that experience for every believer.

The Early Church often experienced such signs and wonders as divine healing, miraculous deliverance, and the casting out of devils. After Jesus gave the Great Commission—"Go ye into all the world, and preach the gospel to every creature" (Mark 16:15)—He continued by saying, "And these signs shall follow them that believe; In my name shall they cast out devils; they shall speak with new tongues; they shall take up serpents; and if they drink any deadly thing, it shall not hurt them; they shall lay hands on the sick, and they shall recover" (verses 17–18). Some early manuscripts of Mark do not contain that passage, but there can be no doubt that it came from a time when people were still living who had heard what Jesus said. It is common with ancient manuscripts to lose the first or last pages. Besides, the passage was written in the same style and vocabulary as the rest of the Gospel of Mark.

Let us not go looking for devils to cast out, but when the need arises let us have the power to control evil spirits in the name of Jesus. The more we walk in the light, the greater will be our conflict with the darkness.

Jesus said that believers would speak with other tongues. It was to be a sign of the true Christian. Even if there were no other passage in the Bible on speaking with other tongues, this one from Jesus would be sufficient.

As for taking up serpents or drinking poison, Jesus was promising supernatural protection for those who face life-threatening dangers from nature or human treachery . . . in the process of carrying out the Great Commission.[*]

Finally, divine healing by the laying on of hands was to be a major Christian activity. The healing of the sick was prominent in the ministry of Jesus and in that of His first followers and must continue to hold that place of prominence in our ministries today. If Jesus thought He needed divine healing to support His ministry, how do we think we will succeed with anything less? We must ask, In how many of our churches are pastors regularly laying hands on the sick?

Yes, the Early Church was experience-oriented, and Pentecostal Christians need to continue that emphasis today. People need to be saved, not just brought into the friendliness of our congregations. They need to be filled with the Holy Spirit and speak with other tongues, not merely identify themselves with a Pentecostal church. They need to be healed, not always ushered into Christian counseling to learn to cope with their disability. And some of them need to have devils cast out of them.

Pentecostal Practices

Our Lord established two ordinances in the church, water baptism and Communion. Water baptism is to follow repentance and is intended both as a ceremonial washing and as a personal identification with the death and resurrection of Jesus Christ, "in the name of the Father, and of the Son, and of the Holy Ghost" (Matthew 28:19). Communion is the table of the Lord around which all Christians must meet in identification with the broken body and shed blood of our Lord. Jesus said, "This do in remembrance of me" (Luke 22:19). We should not experiment with these ordinances but do them simply in their scriptural purity.

---

[*]In foreign missionary service in Colombia, David Womack was healed of poisonings on at least three occasions, although Colombian Christians claim there were more. Some of the people who administered the poison were converted to Christ after seeing the poison had no effect and testify of these events in the churches today.

In addition to these, there were other practices of the Early Church:

1. *They met together in the Upper Room and in the temple.* They "continued steadfastly in the apostles' doctrine and fellowship" (Acts 2:42). They also, "continuing daily with one accord in the temple, and breaking bread from house to house, did eat their meat with gladness and singleness of heart, praising God, and having favor with all the people" (2:46–47). The apostle Paul said, "Not forsaking the assembling of ourselves together, as the manner of some is; but exhorting one another" (Hebrews 10:25).

The services of the Early Church were intense meetings where the needs of the people were met by the miraculous power of God and the Word of God was preached with authority.

2. *They were in prayer and supplication.* Here we have the basis for the Pentecostal manner of praying out loud and in unison. Prayer is talking with God, for when the disciples asked Jesus to teach them to pray He taught them words, "Our Father which art in heaven . . . " (Matthew 6:9). On the other hand, to supplicate is to ask earnestly and humbly. It has to do with emotional intensity and attitude. "Prayer and supplication" is prayer with earnest intensity and humility behind it. This form of earnest prayer is typically Pentecostal.

3. *They preached.* Peter preached on the Day of Pentecost, before the Jewish authorities, and at the house of Cornelius. Stephen preached before the Greek-speaking "synagogue of the Libertines" (freed slaves). Paul preached wherever he went. In most cases, the sermons (or homilies, as they were called) generally took the form of referring to the Scriptures and applying them to the current situation or condition—a style revived in Pentecostal preaching today.

4. *They gave altar calls.* The apostles' sermons called for action by the hearers: repent, be baptized, be filled with the Spirit (Acts 2:38). Their preaching produced results. It only makes sense that sermons that call for action should provide an opportunity for the hearers to respond.

The Early Church did not have church sanctuaries, pulpits, or altar benches; nevertheless, in their meetings they repented of their sins, were baptized, experienced the wind and fire of the Spirit, were filled with the Holy Spirit and spoke in other tongues, felt the room shake, confronted sin and deception, and received God's direction for their lives. The church service was a dynamic event in which Spirit-filled people met with God and expected supernatural things to happen. Every case of speaking in tongues described in the Bible took place in a Christian meeting. It was in that setting that "the Lord added to the church daily such as should be saved" (Acts 2:47).

5. *They practiced water baptism and Communion.* They practiced faithfully both those ordinances. Every Christian was to be baptized once and receive Communion regularly. We Pentecostals are often very informal in our worship, but we should take seriously the ordinances of baptism and Communion and treat them with the degree of ceremony and respect they deserve.

6. *They believed for healing and cast out devils.* The first Christians placed much emphasis on the miraculous. Although it had the effect of attracting people to their message, in most cases these Christians believed for miracles because of compassion or because the situation called for a supernatural sign. Peter and John said to the lame man at the temple gate, "In the name of Jesus Christ of Nazareth rise up and walk" (Acts 3:6). (Notice they did not pray for the sick man but spoke to the person!) Afterward, they prayed to God, "By stretching forth thine hand to heal; and that signs and wonders may be done by the name of thy holy child Jesus" (Acts 4:30).

So great were the manifestations of the power of God that "they brought forth the sick into the streets, and laid them on beds and couches, that at least the shadow of Peter passing by might overshadow some of them. There came also a multitude out of the cities round about Jerusalem, bringing sick folks, and them which were vexed with unclean spirits: and they were healed every one" (Acts 5:15–16).

Pentecostal Priorities

The first instruction to the Early Church was to be filled with the Holy Spirit. Jesus told His apostles, "Behold, I send the promise of my Father upon you: but tarry ye in the city of Jerusalem, until ye be endued with power from on high" (Luke 24:49). They were not to leave the city before being baptized in the Holy Spirit.

Another priority was prayer. Apostolic prayer was generally accompanied by some other word, such as "supplication" or "fasting." In preparation for Pentecost, the first believers were in "prayer and supplication" (Acts 1:14). The first Christians "continued steadfastly in the apostles' doctrine and fellowship, and in breaking of bread, and in prayers" (Acts 2:42). Acts 13:2 says the church in Antioch "ministered to the Lord [worshiped], and fasted," and in the next verse they "fasted and prayed." We cannot overestimate the connection between Pentecostal power and Pentecostal prayer and fasting!

The greatest priority (for which these others were the preparation) was evangelism—preaching the gospel. Jesus said, "But ye shall receive power, after that the Holy Ghost is come upon you: and ye shall be witnesses unto me" (Acts 1:8).

The more like the Early Church we are, the greater will be our commitment to this challenge. Our first priority must be the salvation of the lost. Even on the Day of Pentecost when the 120 were busy speaking with other tongues, Peter looked up at the gathering multitude, switched back into the common Aramaic language, preached the gospel, and saw three thousand people converted.

Yet another priority was the second coming of Jesus Christ. This was what gave the Early Church its urgency. Paul said, "Then we which are alive and remain shall be caught up . . . to meet the Lord" (1 Thessalonians 4:17). Christ did not come in their lifetime; apparently they did not understand how many people "every creature" was or how far from them "the uttermost part of the earth" was. The Early Church could not have foreseen the centuries of backslidden Christianity or an age that would reject the very Pentecostal nature that gave them their power.

A Pentecostal Revival

There is no middle ground between being Pentecostal and relating to some other form of Christianity. We must not even attempt to be marginally Pentecostal, for there are no biblical options short of full commitment to the original model. Either we *are* Pentecostal or we *are not* Pentecostal.

We must not allow the critics, the compromisers, or the confused to talk us out of our Pentecostal faith. We must not allow the counterfeits, the charlatans, and the frauds who have abused and made a mockery of Pentecostal power to deter us from doing what we ought to do and being what we ought to be.

We must not join those debilitating, last-day forces whom the apostle Paul described as "having a form of godliness, but denying the power thereof" (2 Timothy 3:5). There is one true Christianity, and that is original, apostolic, New Testament, Pentecostal Christianity.

For too long the church has sat seething in the melting pot of this world, becoming ever softer year after year and taking on the flavor of the world's ungodly stew. It is time to get the church out of the world and the world out of the church. Never before have we faced a greater need for a generation of revived, restored, and radical revolutionaries for Jesus Christ.

There is no such thing as being a little bit Pentecostal. If you're going to be Pentecostal, accept it wholeheartedly and completely, but don't adopt a Pentecostal style without a commitment to Pentecostal power. Allow the freedom of the Spirit (freedom of response to the Spirit) and a wide range of opportunities for people to respond. High congregational participation is absolutely necessary for an effective Pentecostal service.

We cannot just decide to be Pentecostal, because it is more than a choice; it is an event. Only with a fresh outpouring of the Holy Spirit will we experience the revival we seek.

In a message titled "A Call to Revival," Oklahoma District Superintendent Armon Newburn captured the very heart of this call to revival:

> What is revival? Revival is a mighty spiritual awakening among the people of God that will turn their hearts toward God as they earnestly seek His divine will for their lives. This turning to God and seeking God will produce a people sanctified, set apart, holy living, and completely obedient to the Word of God. This obedience to the will and Word of God will cause the church to thrust in the sickle and reap the ripened harvest of lost souls for whom Christ gave His precious blood.

In his book *Great Revivals,* Colin C. Whittaker wrote of "the fourth R." Rather than the educational version of "Readin', 'Ritin', and 'Rithmetic," he referred to "Reformation" (doctrine), "Renewal" (dynamics), and "Restoration" (direction), to which he added the fourth "R" of "Revival."

At the turn of the past century God gave us a wonderful Pentecostal revival that changed the world; and now we ask Him to close this century and begin the next with an even greater visitation of His Holy Spirit.

8

A Return to Holiness

There is a subject that has been an embarrassment to Pentecostal people, so much so that we hesitate to mention it aloud. We cringe when we hear it preached and pass over it when we read of it. That subject is holiness, and we display little more interest in its companion, righteousness.

Perhaps it is because many of us have thought we came out of the Holiness movement, and having turned our back upon it we do not wish to discuss it further. What an awful mistake! The Pentecostal movement was not a departure from the Holiness movement but rather its most natural and logical fulfillment. An emphasis on holiness was necessary before there could be an outpouring of the Holy Spirit, and it will be required again for any new Pentecostal awakening.

We had planned to call this chapter "A Revival of Righteousness," thinking of *holiness* and *righteousness* as near synonyms, but as we pored over the Word of God in prayer and with open hearts, we discovered a great difference between the two words. In the New Testament they represent two quite different concepts. Luke 1:75 speaks of "holiness and righteousness before him, all the days of our life." Romans 6:19 mentions "righteousness unto holiness." In Ephesians 4:24, Paul wrote, "Put on the new man, which after God is created in righteousness and true holiness." It became clear that righteousness and holiness are different biblical concepts based on separate Greek words. Indeed, righteousness is a necessary precursor to holiness.

On the other hand, in the New Testament, "holiness" and "sanctification" are different translations of the same Greek word (*hagiasmós*, from the root word *hagnós*, "pure") and thus mean the same thing. To be *holy*, or *sanctified*, is to be "ceremonially or morally clean" and thus set apart from anything common or unclean.

Of course, we have problems with "sanctified," too, because some of our early Pentecostals and most of our friends in the Holiness movement made the mistake of thinking of sanctification as a second definite work of grace, as if the blood of Jesus were insufficient at salvation to bring death to the old man and life to the new. Besides, their claim that their sinful nature had been rooted out did not jibe with their testimony. There is a humility in choosing a holy life-style and an arrogance in thinking we cannot sin. A knowledge of our own vulnerability is a major driving force of holiness. Another related word is *saint*, which refers to a godly person who lives a holy life. There are a number of other similar words, such as *sanctify, purification, purity, justice, justification, equity,* and all are related to holiness or righteousness.

The Way of Holiness

It is no wonder that we do not know what holiness is, because our whole society has failed to grasp it. A dictionary defines *holiness* as "the quality of being holy; sanctity" or "a title of address used for the pope." For *holy* it gives "of or associated with a divine power or religious beliefs and traditions; spiritually pure; saintly" and "worthy of special respect or awe." Yes, *holiness* is used in these ways, but our popular definitions do not mention God or approach the meaning of the Hebrew and Greek words so translated in our Bible.

In the Old Testament, the Hebrew word for "holiness" was *qôdesh*, from *qâdash*: "to be holy, separated from ordinary use, dedicated to the service of the Lord." Paul S. Rees said, "The root idea of the Hebrew word, religiously viewed, is that of withdrawal and consecration: withdrawal from what is common or unclean, consecration to what is divine, sacred, pure." Thus, holiness always involves separation—detached from the world

91

and set apart for God. The clearest example of such holiness was the temple vessels, which were consecrated solely for religious use and were not to be profaned by any common or worldly contact.

"Holy" and "holiness" appear more than 830 times in the Old Testament. For example, Isaiah wrote, "And a highway shall be there, and a way, and it shall be called The way of holiness; the unclean shall not pass over it" (Isaiah 35:8). Another great holiness verse is 1 Chronicles 16:29, "Give unto the Lord the glory due unto his name: bring an offering, and come before him: worship the Lord in the beauty of holiness."

As we have seen, the New Testament word for "holiness" is *hagiasmós*, also translated "sanctification." "Holy" is *hágios* ("pure"). For example, Paul wrote, "But now being made free from sin, and become servants to God, ye have your fruit unto holiness, and the end everlasting life" (Romans 6:22). In 2 Corinthians 7:1, he said, "Having therefore these promises, dearly beloved, let us cleanse ourselves from all filthiness of the flesh and spirit, perfecting holiness in the fear of God." Or, there is 1 Thessalonians 3:13, "To the end he may stablish your hearts unblamable in holiness before God, even our Father, at the coming of our Lord Jesus Christ with all his saints." In 1 Thessalonians 4:7, Paul said, "For God hath not called us unto uncleanness, but unto holiness." Hebrews 12:10 speaks of our being "partakers of his holiness." In these verses we can see the connection between holiness and being clean and saintly. There can be no doubt about it; there is too much about holiness in the Bible for us to continue to ignore this significant subject or to think that it refers only to any historical period of legalism. Since God says, "I am the Lord, I change not" (Malachi 3:6), His expectations of our life-style must not vary with cultures, times, or conditions.

In the light of the worldliness of today's church, we must return to the biblical meaning of holiness and respect the injunction: "Follow peace with all men, and holiness, without which no man shall see the Lord" (Hebrews 12:14). We cannot continue to hang our holiness in the closet and bring it out for church like some Sunday-go-to-meeting garment. A cry for holiness must precede any real revival.

Closely tied to holiness is the equally annoying topic of repentance, even though it is the only door to holiness. We may see the connection between holiness and repentance in the ministry of John the Baptist, who preceded the arrival of Jesus Christ by coming out of the desert, crying, "Repent ye: for the kingdom of heaven is at hand" (Matthew 3:2). John the Baptist was, as prophesied by Isaiah, "the voice of one crying in the wilderness, Prepare ye the way of the Lord, make his paths straight" (verse 3). He did not dress or eat like most other people but dared to be different in the name of the Lord—an idea not foreign to early Pentecostals. We have to wonder if there could have been a John the Baptist if he had been raised on television and in American schools instead of possibly in the harsh classrooms of the Essene sect at Qumran!*

The first step to holiness is repentance, and to have effective repentance we must arouse a new interest in prayer. Isaiah had already been wonderfully used of the Lord, but when he found himself in the presence of Almighty God, he repented of his unclean lips and of the unclean people with whom he associated. Look at the steps of his repentance and subsequent holiness in Isaiah 6:1–8:

1. *He saw the Lord on His throne, high and lifted up.* Any fresh relationship with God will produce an increased awareness of His exaltation and holiness. When we use the word *holiness* for God, we mean that He is completely apart from anything common or unclean.

2. *He experienced the worship of God—"Holy, holy, holy, is the Lord of Hosts"* (verse 3). Notice that "holy" is the major word used for God's praise! We approach God through praise, for Psalm 22:3 says of the Lord, "But thou art holy, O thou that inhabitest the praises of Israel." Isaiah heard the seraphim praising God, saw the doorposts shake in the presence of the Lord, and saw the smoke that filled the room. Supernatural things happen in the presence of the Lord. We must continue to expect that something supernatural will happen in every church service: a healing, a message in prophecy or tongues and interpretation, an anointed sermon, people saved. . . .

---

*Many believe that John the Baptist was a member of the Essenes at Qumran. The Essenes were the people who preserved the Dead Sea Scrolls, including perhaps the very copy of Isaiah used to identify the ministry of John.

3. *He felt guilty in God's presence and repented of his uncleanness.* The inspired prophet already had written five chapters of the Book of Isaiah, but in God's presence he became aware of his sin and need of repentance. Such a need to repent includes all Christians at all levels of position or ministry, "for all have sinned, and come short of the glory of God" (Romans 3:23). Yes, we are justified by faith (verse 24), but practical faith must be reflected in corresponding works. The closer we get to God the more aware we will be of our sins of commission (wrong things we have done), of omission (right things we have failed to do), and of "no-mission" (lack of commitment to divine purpose).

4. *His solution was at the altar.* One of the seraphim touched Isaiah's lips with a live coal taken with tongs from the altar and said, "Thine iniquity is taken away, and thy sin purged" (Isaiah 6:7). This was the altar of incense, representing perpetual prayer or what the apostle Paul called prayer "without ceasing" (Romans 1:9; 1 Thessalonians 2:13; 2 Timothy 1:3; Revelation 8:3).

God can speak to us anywhere, but Pentecostal Christians have a covenant with God to meet Him regularly at the prayer altar, where they find live fire and forgiveness. There is something particularly effective about making a public confession—not publicly denigrating ourselves but going forward in a public service and falling on our knees before God. Holiness results from penitence (remorse for sin to ourselves), repentance (admitting our sin to God), and asking forgiveness (a request God never denies for the sincere supplicant). To know God is to become like Him in a life-style high and lifted up in the beauty of holiness.

5. *Only after his repentance could Isaiah carry out his divine mission.* The Lord asked, "Whom shall I send, and who will go for us?" (Isaiah 6:8). The now holy Isaiah enthusiastically replied, "Here am I; send me," and proceeded to write sixty-one more chapters of the Book of Isaiah, including most of his prophecies about Christ. We cannot do God's work until we become like God.

This is the center of our identity as Christians. The apostle Peter said, "But ye are a chosen generation, a royal priesthood, a holy nation, a peculiar people; that ye should show forth the praises of him who hath called you out of darkness into his marvelous light" (1 Peter 2:9). We are to be a holy, separated people, thoroughly dedicated to the service of our Lord. Although well-intentioned in being God's peculiar people, too often Pentecostals have succeeded in being merely peculiar.

As more and more of our people enter into the presence of God in prayer, we will see a fresh realization of our sinful condition, followed by widespread repentance. Then, as we enter into a new era of holiness, the revival we seek will break out wherever this process occurs.

It was in anticipation of that sequence that General Superintendent Trask and the Executive Presbytery called for a sacred assembly, a gathering of church leaders to fast, pray, repent, and seek God.[*] The idea was based on Joel 2:15 —"Blow the trumpet in Zion, sanctify a fast, call a solemn assembly." However, we must issue a stern warning not to forget that the people of Judah did not listen to the prophet Joel. In a spirit of rebellion and rejection of any call to holiness, they did not blow the trumpet, fast, or call a solemn assembly, and so the enemy came and carried them away to captivity in Babylon.

The Assemblies of God in the last decade of the twentieth century faces many of the same problems that brought on Joel's call for a solemn assembly. The difference is that we are blowing the trumpet and have called for movement-wide repentance. Therefore, we may expect positive and revival-bringing results.

Ezekiel had a vision of water running from under the threshold of the temple and flowing over the dry and thirsty land, causing the waiting soil to bear all kinds of food-producing plants (Ezekiel 47:1–12). At first the water came up to Ezekiel's ankles, but as he continued into the stream it came up to his knees, then his waist, and then over his head in a mighty river that no one could cross. This river of rivers flows from the Holy of Holies, and no real revival will ever begin in any other way.

Paths of Righteousness

If righteousness and holiness are not synonyms, we must learn the difference between them. One dictionary says the word *righteousness* means "morally right; just." So while holiness relates to separation from the world and consecration to

---

[*]The sacred assembly was held in Springfield, Missouri, on March 1–3, 1994.

God, righteousness relates more to humankind. *Righteousness* means "justice, equity, fairness," or "doing what is right."

David Broughton Knox said that "righteousness" is the regular translation of the Hebrew *ts^{e}dâkâh* and the Greek *dikaiosúnē.* "Originally, these words signified that which conforms to the norm. And for biblical writers this norm is the character of God himself." He said of the word "right," "In the NT the chief word is *dikáios*, meaning 'upright.' It is usually translated 'just' or 'right.'"

We see, then, that holiness is separation from the world and unto God, and righteousness is the quality of the believer toward others. This should come as no surprise, for when asked about the greatest commandment, Jesus said, "Thou shalt love the Lord thy God with all thy heart, and with all thy soul, and with all thy mind. This is the first and great commandment. And the second is like unto it, Thou shalt love thy neighbor as thyself. On these two commandments hang all the law and the prophets" (Matthew 22:37–40). Holiness and righteousness—relationship to God and relationship to humankind—comprise the whole message of the Word of God.

Here are a few of the many outstanding verses on righteousness in the Bible:

Psalm 17:15, "I will behold thy face in righteousness: I shall be satisfied, when I awake, with thy likeness."

Psalm 23:3, "He restoreth my soul: he leadeth me in the paths of righteousness for his name's sake."

Hosea 10:12, "Sow to yourselves in righteousness, reap in mercy; break up your fallow ground: for it is time to seek the Lord, till he come and rain righteousness upon you."

Matthew 5:6, "Blessed are they which do hunger and thirst after righteousness: for they shall be filled."

Matthew 6:33, "But seek ye first the kingdom of God, and his righteousness; and all these things shall be added unto you."

1 Corinthians 15:34, "Awake to righteousness, and sin not; for some have not the knowledge of God: I speak this to your shame." These words were written to "the church of God which is at Corinth, to them that are sanctified in Christ Jesus, called to be saints, with all that in every place call upon the name of Jesus Christ our Lord" (1 Corinthians 1:2)!

Ephesians 4:24, "And that ye put on the new man, which after God is created in righteousness and true holiness."

2 Timothy 3:16, "All scripture is given by inspiration of God, and is profitable for doctrine, for reproof, for correction, for instruction in righteousness."

Righteousness is the state of living and doing right, toward God and toward people. It is an absolute necessity for the Christian life, since its absence is a sure sign of ungodliness. If there is unrighteousness among us, let us stop whatever sins we are doing immediately and return to the standards of our righteous God.

What Shall We Do?

Just as it did at the close of Peter's sermon on the Day of Pentecost, there comes a critical moment for godly action: Sinners feel the guilt of their iniquity, and the preacher has a precise moment in which to bring them to Christ. We are at that point now, and we ask with Peter's hearers, "Men and brethren, what shall we do?" (Acts 2:37).

If ever we needed a word of wisdom, it is today. A favorite definition of *wisdom* is "knowing what to do next." We cannot attain holiness by merely trying to be better in our own power, for holiness comes out of an encounter with God. Early Pentecostals often were confused about this, and their legalistic way of life became a bondage rather than the liberty of the Spirit.

In holiness, our motivation comes from a relationship with God. Holy Christians will not do things displeasing to Him because they have no interest in them. One man said, "I didn't give up swearing. I just forgot about it." A person whose mind is on God will have difficulty enjoying a worldly entertainment show because the content grieves his spirit, and he also will think of the poor witness it is for those who may be watching his testimony. Holiness is not a legalistic bondage but a liberating freedom. We are free to do the will of God! Our guilt is gone! We do everything we want to do, but the things we want to do have changed.

So, what are the things that need to change in the Assemblies of God? That is not the important question. What is vital is what God thinks. He is not looking for a long rehearsal of sins He already knows all too well, but He expects sincere repentance and a wholehearted return to His Word.

Yes, we have problems, and many congregations have lowered their standards of holiness until they bear little resemblance to the New Testament church. The answer to our need is not a wallowing in our own guilt but in a heartfelt return to prayer, remorse for sin, repentance, and a fresh relationship with God. Then the Holy Spirit will conduct His own cleanup campaign. It is He who "will reprove the world of sin, and of righteousness, and of judgment" (John 16:8).

When will the revival begin? As far as we and many prayer warriors across this land are concerned, it has begun already. The question is not how to start it but who will join it!

9

How Pentecostal People
Have Church

After a Sunday night service in a charged atmosphere of praise and enthusiasm that included several people being saved, two young people being filled with the Holy Spirit with speaking in other tongues, and a number of believers being healed of various diseases and conditions, an impressed man with tears in his eyes said to the pastor, "We really had church tonight!"

Pentecostal people believe that anyone can have a meeting, but it takes the supernatural moving of the Holy Spirit to "have church."

What Will Happen Next?

We come now to the most dramatic characteristics of Pentecostal Christians. It is here that we are most often questioned and are most apt to disagree with others. Indeed, some of our churches no longer enjoy the blessings of such services or may even have forgotten how to initiate them. Some have ceased to experience such moving of the Spirit because their pastors grew up in spiritually deprived churches and never were taught how to lead in the Spirit.

Even people sympathetic to our perspective tend to think that such services happen only when the Holy Spirit takes over, rather than seeing that God's leader operates in the Spirit and leads the church into an active response to God.

Do you remember Michelangelo's painting of the Sistine Chapel, particularly the finger of God touching the finger of Adam? Something powerful happens when we reach out and touch God, especially when we realize that He is responding by reaching out to us. At the end of the Book of Ezekiel, the enraptured prophet saw the city with twelve gates, which John called the New Jerusalem. In the center of the city was the presence of God, whose name was *Yahweh Shammah*, "The Lord Is There" (Ezekiel 48:35). God is in the midst of His people to touch them and be experienced by them. Jesus said, "For where two or three are gathered together in my name, there am I in the midst of them" (Matthew 18:20). A congregation of believing Spirit-filled people is a flammable condition, and an awareness of the Holy Spirit's presence is the spark that sets a Pentecostal service aflame.

About 1932, Pentecostal writer Donald Gee said,

> I am a little concerned when I find people getting too respectable. They may have fine churches with lovely carpets, pipe organs, and choirs; but I hope the Lord will put the poker into their furnace soon and stir them up. I say this solemnly because the supernatural is beginning to wane in some places. I go to some assemblies where they never have a message in tongues or interpretation, where they have never heard the gift of prophecy, where the meeting is carried on like clockwork, and you always know what will happen next in the program.

Some people see us as a fanatical outgrowth of American revivalism, that the highly emotional evangelistic styles of Dwight L. Moody, Charles Finney, and other preachers led to churches with revivalistic characteristics. Certainly much of our style grew out of our historical background, but the enthusiasm and praise of a Pentecostal service come more from the present experience of the believers than from any tradition. People really are converted, healed, and changed in our services. Once we know that God is present to meet our needs, the supernatural comes quite naturally. God has always responded in power to those who earnestly seek Him.

We believe that God works actively in human affairs, knows us personally, has a purpose for each of us, and will support our ministries for Him with supernatural manifestations. We can see that concept clearly in Mark 16:15–18, where Jesus first told His followers to preach the gospel to everyone everywhere and then promised them supernatural support—casting out devils, speaking in other tongues, miraculous deliverance from natural and human dangers, and healing the sick. When we Pentecostals rediscovered original Christianity, we once again saw New Testament results.

The Threefold Ministry of the Church

Going to church is more than meeting with our friends and gathering to study the Bible and learn Christian values and virtues; it is meeting with the awesome presence of God through Jesus Christ and His Holy Spirit.

The Assemblies of God went through some serious changes in the 1960s. Some people suspected we had lost our way, but the problem was that we were working under an inadequate definition of the church and its mission. We made a detailed self-evaluation that culminated in the 1968 Council on Evangelism in St. Louis, Missouri, and went on to include a new definition in our Statement of Fundamental Truths.

It was one of those why-didn't-we-see-it-till-now revelations. The new definition of our mission was simple, but it revolutionized our thinking and guided us into a new period of growth. Before 1968, if anyone would have asked, "What is the purpose of the church?" we would have said, "Evangelism." There was nothing wrong with that single-minded definition, but it fell short of the whole purpose of the church.

The new definition, elegant in its simplicity and clear in its meaning, became known as the church's threefold mission:

Ministry to the Lord
Ministry to the Church
Ministry to the World

This concept may be illustrated by the cross: The upright points both upward to God and inward to the church as the crosspiece points outward to the world. We may also think of it as the "three ships" of worship, fellowship, and discipleship.

It appears today that we may have gotten out of balance between these three elements. There is less difference now between our worship and that of other evangelical churches, possibly because there is less difference in our experience. We have emphasized internal development, although there is less fellowship between congregations. Concerning discipleship, we talk of it more and do it less than at any time in our history. Much of our evangelism is left to evangelists and missionaries, and we think we have done our part by supporting them. Many of our people do not even attend when an evangelist or missionary is to speak!

The Pentecostal church service is one aspect of the whole life of the church. And because God makes His presence known in such services, people often are affected emotionally. We need to understand that people who weep at the altar, praise God out loud, and get emotional in church are not a problem to us but rather our only hope. Revival is our survival! These people who "enter in" to a service and yield to the Holy Spirit are the same ones who give many hours a week teaching Sunday school classes, working in youth ministries, developing children through Missionettes and Royal Rangers, singing in the choir, working as ushers, feeding the hungry, caring for the homeless, and mowing church lawns—all the while holding down full-time jobs and tithing!

Pentecostal people are not just starry-eyed dreamers with their heads in the clouds; they are down-to-earth, extremely practical people who believe that God still is active in the lives of ordinary people. You might say they are spiritual pragmatists. There are no more active, practical Christians in the world than Pentecostals. Just look at all their successful programs, the size of many of their largest churches, their number of Bible colleges and institutes, and their worldwide missions programs. Yes indeed, those people with their hands in the air, their knees on the floor, or lying prostrate before God are as inspired in their practical service as they are in their church services. The old saying "He's so heavenly minded that he's no earthly good" just isn't true; heavenly minded people have done the most earthly good . . . often to the uttermost places of the earth!

Many of us have observed that some people who are demonstrative at the altar may not show equal interest in the practical work of the church. Yet, Christ intended that Spirit-filled people should be His witnesses (Acts 1:8). On the Day of Pentecost the 120 had a highly demonstrative experience of the baptism in the Holy Spirit, and yet when they saw the multitudes gather they stopped speaking in tongues and preached the gospel.

For readers who have not experienced what many Pentecostals call "having church," we offer the following explanation. It is not our intention to criticize anyone but rather to offer a model of what to expect in your church when the coming revival breaks forth.

A Pentecostal Church Service

Churches vary so greatly that it would be impossible to describe a typical service. In the same city there will be an uptown church that is reaching the upper middle class or higher, a downtown church whose congregation is from the emerging middle class or lower, and several ethnolinguistic* churches that minister to specific cultures and language groups. Churches may be sophisticated or country . . . or sophisticated country. Every church is different. Additionally, every church is in flux, its life constantly changing as people and their spiritual conditions come and go. Some churches seem to be on fire, while, as T. C. Cunningham[†] was fond of saying, "Some churches are so dry they constitute a fire hazard."

Yet, there are identifying similarities of Pentecostal church services. Most open with what they call the song service, which leads to congregational prayer. After that, there will be some announcements, the receiving of an offering, some special music, and the sermon. Of course, any churchgoing American will immediately recognize that nearly all evangelical churches fit that description. Pentecostal churches differ not so much in what they do as in how they do it: The singing is enthusiastic and may be accompanied by handclapping and open praise. Many churches have both a piano and an organ, but there may be other instruments, from a set of drums to a complete orchestra. With the growing number of electronic instruments and equipment, some churches no longer use the traditional piano and organ but accompany their singing with synthesizers or

---

*In search of a convenient word to describe its many cultural and language-group churches, the Northern California–Nevada District adopted "ethnolinguistic." We Pentecostals not only speak in tongues but sometimes are unintelligible in our own language.

[†]T. C. Cunningham served for many years as assistant district superintendent and world missions director for the Southern California District. He was often called "Mister Missions."

orchestral sound tracks on cassette tapes, compact disks, or the newer digital computer disks. As we increase our uses of high-technology equipment, we must be careful not to lose our Pentecostal spontaneity.

In addition to the songs in the hymnal, the church may sing shorter praise songs called choruses, often our most distinctive music. Yet, our Pentecostal distinctiveness in this area also is being lost as a few companies own the copyrights and produce sound tracks and projection transparencies that are so generic that they may be used in any church of any persuasion.

We might repeat a chorus or the refrain of a favorite hymn over and over as the congregation enters into expressions of praise. Church music certainly is intended to glorify the Lord, but it also provides other benefits. For example, having everyone sing together with the same words and rhythm produces the effect of leaving behind the cares and concerns of the outside world and entering into corporate worship. Most music in the world today has a few people performing before an audience of listeners and spectators. Not so with Pentecostal church music, for our singing is highly participatory and intended to bring the individual into group involvement in the service. Our music unites us and our thinking in a worshiping body of believers.

Another benefit is that, since most of our music is very specific to the culture being reached, the singing attracts new people to the services and is a powerful tool of evangelism. By the same token, people who are not of a given culture may not find the music to their liking and may seek a church of their own background. For example, in areas of the country where people of European heritage predominate, one is likely to find traditional Protestant hymns, few instruments other than piano and organ (unless they have an orchestra), and choirs singing anthems. In most metropolitan areas, where congregations may be made up of other races or of mixed heritage, one will find tambourines, drums, rhythm-style piano, contemporary organ, electric bass guitars, and choirs singing what they call soul music. We may add to this the great number of country churches with their drums, guitars, basses, violins, and distinctive manner of singing. In many areas of the country there are churches of other cultures where Spanish, Korean, Tongan, Samoan, Fijian, Vietnamese, Chinese, or other people each will have their own distinctive music. Adaptability to language and culture is one of the hallmarks of the Pentecostal movement. It began on the Day of Pentecost and continues wherever the Holy Spirit is allowed to interact with a congregation. This is one of the reasons for our continued success in world missions.

The high level of enthusiastic participation continues into the prayer time. Pentecostal people usually stand and pray out loud, and the person leading in prayer begins only when the sounds of congregational praise have ebbed. This practice may confuse or even frighten those not accustomed to hearing people lift up their voices aloud to God. During prayer, or at any time in the service, people may raise their hands as a physical expression of praise.

Most pastors have tried to shorten the announcements, but when activities go unannounced they also go unattended. Sunday bulletins help, but our many announcements are witnesses to the number of activities and ministries in our churches. As for our offerings, many of our people tithe ten percent of their income and give additional offerings to support world missions and other ministries. Some churches even applaud at the mention of an offering.

Music and the Message

There was a time when our music was more distinctive than it is today, because people often wrote their own songs and accompanied themselves on the piano or guitar. Some even sang solos to the tambourine! It wasn't very professional, but it expressed the unique faith of the individual. However, with the popularity of gospel music today and the advent of background tapes, this uniqueness is changing. There is little individuality and the same sounds will be heard in any church or on television, radio, or recordings. The music is better, but something intimate is being lost. There is a ray of hope, because the majority of today's gospel musicians are growing up in highly participatory, Pentecostal churches. Yet, there was something much more personal when church music had no electric cords, no sound system, and caused no vibrations in the sanctuary floor. When we made a mistake, we called it a "hallelujah breakdown."

A distinguishing Pentecostal trait is that at almost any time in the service—except when someone is leading, singing, or preaching—a person might break out with a message in prophecy or speak forth in other tongues, the latter followed by an equally inspired interpretation. There are abuses, but Spirit-filled people know when the message is from God. It concerns us greatly that some pastors discourage praise in tongues or manifesting the gifts of the Spirit in church. Where else should we expect spiritual manifestations to occur? A church service is a live meeting with the living God!

Anointed Preaching

Next comes the sermon. The kind of content and delivery that Pentecostal people call "anointed preaching" has an unmistakable intensity and inspiration to it. Peter's sermon at Pentecost was an extemporaneous message backed by ten days of prayer and supplication, a church in one accord, the baptism in the Holy Spirit, speaking in other tongues, and a lifelong exposure to the Scriptures. We need a revival of that kind of preaching today!

Most early Pentecostal preachers made their preparation in prayer and took to the pulpit only sketchy notes to give a general structure to their sermons. Thus, under the heavy anointing of the Holy Spirit, they were able to establish an intuitive relationship with both God and their hearers and often come right in on people's thoughts and concerns. Preaching was a supernatural event.

Much of today's preaching, unfortunately, is centered on the most selfish aspects of human lives, a reflection of the Me Generation. Yes, we must have compassion for the hurting, but rather than a lecture on human nature or a public counseling session, what they need is to hear more from God's Word and less from the psychology books. The apostle Paul demanded of Timothy, "Preach the word; be instant in season, out of season; reprove, rebuke, exhort with all long-suffering and doctrine" (2 Timothy 4:2). Psalm 107:20 says, "He sent his word, and healed them, and delivered them from their destructions."

Preaching is intended to be intense and spoken right from the heart of God. Anointed preaching is serious business; woe to those charlatans who come to us in the "form of godliness, but denying the power thereof" (2 Timothy 3:5). Every full-gospel preacher faces the terrible temptation to put on a highly motivational, personality-centered show rather than hearing from God and delivering His Word with an anointed and authoritative intensity. Spirit-filled people know the difference, and when we have enough of them to control the compromisers and the nerve-end folks, those who want only emotional stimulation, we will once again have a Holy Ghost revival.

We hear complaints of sermons being too long, especially when the listener wants to get out of church at an anticipated time . . . and when the sermon could have been preached in fewer words with more effect. However, when the preacher is truly anointed by the Holy Spirit, no one wants him to stop at thirty minutes. There are limits to our endurance, but in a revived church the sermons will generally be longer. In a revived Pentecostal church we are hearing from God through the preaching of His Word.

The Altar Call

Where our services differ greatly from those of most other churches is in what happens after the sermon. Just when some people think the pastor is about to dismiss the service, he calls people to the front of the church. Since we believe that people experience salvation at a particular time and place, the pastor may begin by giving an invitation for anyone to accept Jesus Christ as Savior and Lord. In a revived church, where people are excited about their own salvation and talking to others about it, there often will be people who respond to such an altar call.

On a Sunday morning the service might end with the salvation appeal, but come back to a revived church on Sunday night and you may find that the altar service begins about halfway through the meeting. The preacher may call the congregation to kneel at the altar or may have everyone stand and pray together. The pastor and others may pray for the sick and believe for their healing. Believers may be filled with the Holy Spirit and speak in other tongues. There may be prophecies or messages in tongues and interpretation. The Pentecostal movement may have feet to go around the world, but its heart is at the altar.

The more revived the church, the more apt it will be to have altar benches where people may kneel for prayer. The area often will be supplied with boxes of tissues, cushions for those who have trouble kneeling, bottles of anointing oil, and even prayer cloths to cover the legs of ladies and girls who may pray prostrate on the floor. Are these things foreign to today's churches? They won't be in the new spiritual awakening of the next revival.

If your church has not made adequate provision for people to pray at the front of the church, we suggest an immediate remodeling program. Enlarge your altar! Did not Jesus say, "My house shall be called the house of prayer" (Matthew 21:13)? Then, let's make it a place of prayer! Include altar benches with plenty of room for ministry to those who linger there. Many Pentecostal Christians feel that a week is lost that does not begin with a powerful Sunday night service and a loving session with Jesus at the altar.

In the Old Testament, there were two altars, that of sacrifice as the place of salvation and that of incense as the holy place of prayer. Our Christian place of sacrifice for sin is the cross of our Lord Jesus Christ, who was the last and ultimate Sacrifice. In Matthew 5:23–24, Jesus spoke of bringing our gifts to the altar—"If thou bring thy gift to the altar, and there rememberest that thy brother hath aught against thee; leave there thy gift before the altar, and go thy way; first be reconciled to thy brother, and then come and offer thy gift." Therefore, Jesus' concept of the altar was something more than a place of sacrifice. It was to be a place of commitment and prayer. In Revelation 8:3, an angel has a golden censer that he is to offer "with the prayers of all saints upon the golden altar which was before the throne." That represented the altar of incense, where the priests offered prayer before the throne of God, which sat behind the veil in the Holy of Holies. Pentecostal churches have associated that concept and place of prayer with the area before the pulpit. The Word of God comes forth from the pulpit area, and in front of that is the place of prayer.

Pentecostal churches often play music during the altar service, and as people end their prayers someone might lead them in singing. This is a biblical idea, since Psalm 43:4 says, "Then will I go unto the altar of God, unto God my exceeding joy: yea, upon the harp will I praise thee, O God my God." Many Pentecostal Christians find great personal satisfaction in such singing after prayer at the altar.

A Pentecostal church that does not have what we call altar

services, does not lay hands on the sick, or does not listen to the voice of the Lord in messages in prophecy or tongues and interpretation really isn't committed to being Pentecostal. We may fear that such things will drive people away, but experience has shown us over and over again that live Pentecostal churches grow, and dull churches fade away. If your church is lacking in the power of the Spirit, go to your knees in prayer until that touch of God is on your ministry.

A Matter for Thought

Over the past few years an increasing number of pastors have introduced a prayer time early in the service when people come forward to the altar for prayer. Some feel that this time of personal attention at the altar might be better placed after the preaching of the Word, which is intended to instruct, inspire, and instill faith in the believer.

General Treasurer James K. Bridges wrote the following expression on this subject:

> I have been concerned with a practice used by many pastors today in which people are called forward to the altar for prayer prior to the preaching of the Word. My concern is in the time in the service when this practice is done. I have watched the growing attitude that makes an altar call after the message seem anticlimactic, to the extent that some pastors have stopped giving altar calls after their message.

> It is a tragedy for a pastor to feel that his message is complete in just the delivery of the sermon. This makes preaching an end in itself. The Holy Spirit never intended this, for preaching must always be a means to an end. A gospel message requires a response, and the altar call must be seen as a vitally important conclusion to the sermon.

> When people feel they have already "gone to the altar" and made their response before the message, then the preaching no longer occurs in anticipation of experience to come.

> My plea is for our preachers to hold the altar call to its rightful place following an anointed message from the Word of God. Allow the altar prayer to be unrestricted. Use elders and deacons, if desired, to assist in prayer, but let the one who has preached be directly involved.

> I see very few people receiving the baptism in the Holy Spirit or being saved in the premessage altar calls that are common today. We must get our altar services back to the place where

people are giving the time necessary to really meet God and make truly spiritual responses to the Word of God and the moving of the Holy Spirit. This is what Pentecost is all about!

A Pentecostal church service is a meeting of Jesus Christ with His bride, the Church. If we become emotional when we know He is there, if we pray too loudly, if we break into tears of joy or of sorrow for sin, if we get too physical, if we act differently in the awareness of the moving of the Holy Spirit than we do anywhere else, if we shout "Hallelujah!" (from Hebrew for "Praise the Lord!"), or speak in other tongues . . . it is because we are not acting out some old tradition but responding sincerely and spontaneously to the very real and personal presence of the Lord. This is the single most important factor in understanding Pentecostal church services: The Lord Is There!

10

Praise and Worship

There are many distinctive characteristics of the Pentecostal movement, but the one that most attracts new people into our churches is our style of worship. Our enthusiastic singing; vocal praise; out-loud prayers; lively choral, solo, and instrumental music; intense preaching; and fervent manner of praying at the altar set our services apart from most other churches.

One thing that visitors notice is that our hands are always busy—greeting one another with a warm handshake, clapping our hands as a sign of praise to God or in appreciation for someone's ministry or testimony, raising our hands in worship, or folding them respectfully in prayer. We also lay hands on the sick and pray for their healing.

An older Pentecostal lady and her charismatic friend were discussing the proper way to hold the hands when raising them before the Lord and could not agree about the right position. The Pentecostal raised her hands with the palms outward, and the charismatic held hers upward. At last the charismatic said, "If you hold your palms outward, you push away the blessing, and if you hold them upward you receive the blessing." She was wrong, of course, for hand positions have no bearing on the receptivity of the heart, but yet this story illustrates that raising our hands as an act of worship is a common practice among all Spirit-filled people.

The Early Church would have followed the Jewish practice of extending the hands outward with the palms up. In the Middle

111

Ages, people in prayer would cross their arms over their chest; monks in southern Europe invented the pretzel with its crossed pieces in the center as a reward for children who said their prayers. Later, Christians pressed their palms together, finger to finger and thumb to thumb, just below the chin, much as in the well-known painting *Praying Hands*. We still might see any of those positions but are more apt to extend our hands upward. Without doubt the Lord looks on the heart, and yet we place much value on assuming a position reserved for prayer and praise.

Worshiping God is an intimate and extremely personal matter. Some people are vocal and unrestrained in their expressions to God, while others feel that their relationship to Him is so personal that they may hesitate to include others in what to them is a highly private matter. There are many dedicated and spiritual Christians in the whole range of expressions from loud to quiet and from demonstrative to reserved. In fact, the provision for a wide variety of responses is one of the reasons Pentecostals believe in what they call the "altar service," where praying out loud, shouting, whispering, or silently listening before the Lord are all in acceptable order.

One thing will nearly always be found in a revived Pentecostal church: Praise will be expressed both spiritually and physically. People unaccustomed to such a full involvement in worship may be uneasy or even embarrassed by the intensity of such praise; but the Bible teaches and Pentecostal people insist that only wholehearted participation in worship is pleasing to God. We often say, "Amen!" "Praise the Lord!" or "Hallelujah!" And there is apt to be handclapping, raised hands, kneeling, or even lying prostrate before the Lord. Let us explore some biblical reasons behind these distinctive Pentecostal practices.

Body, Soul, and Spirit

We must distinguish between scriptural worship as a standard for everyone and cultural and social patterns that may change with times and places. A major strength of the Pentecostal movement is our ability to appeal to and work among people of different social, cultural, and economic classes. Yet, the customs of participatory praise and physical involvement in spiritual worship are common to all Pentecostal people.

According to Genesis 2:7, "the Lord God formed man of the dust of the ground, and breathed into his nostrils the breath of life; and man became a living soul." When God created man, He made his body from the dust of the earth (physical matter) and breathed into him the breath of life (spirit).* Thus, we are both body and spirit, both physical and spiritual. Then, when God had combined matter and spirit in His creation, "man became a living soul." The soul, or psyche, is not an entity in itself but results from the interaction of matter and spirit. God made us from physical materials of earth and breathed His heavenly Spirit into us, and we *became* living souls. We are body, soul, and spirit, with soul listed in the middle because it results from the blending of the other two. The soul, or psyche, is that in us which psychologists can study—our emotions, behavior, and personality traits. God is a triune being, composed of Father, Son, and Holy Spirit; we are triune creatures, composed of the physical, the spiritual, and the psychological (behavioral and emotional).

Jesus said, "Thou shalt love the Lord thy God with all thy heart, and with all thy soul, and with all thy mind" (Matthew 22:37). Here again, in different order, are our responses to God with all three elements of our nature. Mark 12:30 and Luke 10:27 add "strength," increasing the emphasis on physical expressions in worship.

If indeed we are body, soul, and spirit, then our worship to God ought to be physical, emotional, and spiritual. Physical (body) worship may be anything from just being present in church to responding to the presence of God by raising or clapping our hands, saying "amen" or "hallelujah," kneeling at an altar, or even spontaneous dancing in the Spirit.† Emotional

---

*Both *rûach* in Hebrew and *pneûma* in Greek meant "wind," "breath," or "spirit." We may see this in Jesus' conversation with Nicodemus—"The wind bloweth where it listeth, and thou hearest the sound thereof, but canst not tell whence it cometh, and whither it goeth: so is every one that is born of the Spirit" (John 3:8).

†Dancing in the Spirit—movements of the body generally involving the feet—must always be spontaneous, is never sensual, and occurs during times of intense awareness of the presence of God as an expression of praise. It is to be distinguished from planned or choreographed dancing, which is "of the flesh" and has no place in Pentecostal services.

(soul) worship may include singing, responding to gospel music, weeping or laughing before the Lord, or expressing the whole range of human feelings in a great variety of ways. Sometimes people respond to crowd psychology (the group working of the human psyche), and it takes spiritual discernment to know the difference between what is of God and what is merely human. Spiritual (spirit) worship may be an inner communion between our spirit and the Spirit of God, the mental or intellectual aspects of worship, or deep experiences such as visions, trances, or what we Pentecostals called being "lost in the Spirit." When it is truly of God, falling (what we call "slain in the Spirit") may occur when a person becomes so aware of the realm of the Spirit that he or she yields wholly to God and apparently forgets to maintain balance and a standing position. We do not attempt to understand it all, but we have seen many beneficial, life-changing results of such experiences.

Always, there is a great responsibility upon worship leaders to be sincere, directed by the Holy Spirit, and devoid of personal motives for gain or power. Yet, from such a base of humility and selflessness, they must operate in the authority of the Spirit to take control of anything wrong, encourage anything right, and operate in the name of the Lord. The Bible gives excellent rules for such worship in 1 Corinthians 12 through 14. In group worship, it is only in an atmosphere of confidence in the worship leader that the most intense spiritual experiences will occur. The spiritual leader must take charge without taking over, allow for a wide range of human responses, and yet keep the worship oriented toward pleasing God rather than deteriorating into self-gratification. Pentecostal people may enjoy their worship, but the attention must always be centered on God's pleasure rather than their own. With the passing of generations, fewer and fewer of our pastors know how to lead altar services with divine authority without inserting themselves between the people and the Lord. Like milk bottles, they must contain and give direction to human responses without limiting the people's natural desires for God or impeding the flow of the supernatural working of the Spirit.

Pentecostal worship involves the whole person—body, soul, and spirit. We believe in open response to God with our whole being, yielding everything to God, holding back nothing. Although this attitude has often produced unexpected, or even undesirable, effects, the benefits of our open worship have been so great that we have continued to encourage a full response to God. Much of our worldwide success has come from the unlimited, do-or-die commitments of people converted or raised in this atmosphere of wholehearted, fervent yielding to the moving of the Holy Spirit.

If we are to revive original Christianity, we must continue our commitment to open worship with body, soul, and spirit. We must warn, however, that open Pentecostal worship can survive only in an atmosphere of deep spirituality, unselfish motivation, and honest humility. People in such worship are extremely vulnerable to the whims and manipulations of the worship leader or to their own selfish motivations. For this reason more than any other, many pastors have become fearful and have drawn their congregations back from a full response to the Spirit of God. Pentecostal worship requires an open and unlimited exchange between God and His people. Isaiah said, "For thus saith the high and lofty One that inhabiteth eternity, whose name is Holy; I dwell in the high and holy place, with him also that is of a contrite and humble spirit, to revive the spirit of the humble, and to revive the heart of the contrite ones" (Isaiah 57:15).

Notice these passages on praise:

Psalm 9:11, "Sing praises to the Lord, which dwelleth in Zion: declare among the people his doings."

Psalm 22:3, "But thou art holy, O thou that inhabitest the praises of Israel."

Psalm 108:3, "I will praise thee, O Lord, among the people: and I will sing praises unto thee among the nations."

1 Peter 2:9, "But ye are a chosen generation, a royal priesthood, a holy nation, a peculiar people; that ye should show forth the praises of him who hath called you out of darkness into his marvelous light."

Pentecostal worship is participatory and expressive. It is demonstrated physically, emotionally, and spiritually. As the spiritual atmosphere of a church wanes, worship tends to become ceremonial and quiet; however, as revival increases, the worship will become more spontaneous and will be expressed more vocally and physically. These are not learned responses, for they often are most prevalent in the newest converts.

Is There a Difference?

A common phrase in Pentecostal circles today is "praise and worship." The two words often are used together or interchangeably as if they were synonymous with adoration of God. Early Pentecostal worship was quite individual, for it centered on personal experiences with God for salvation, the baptism in the Holy Spirit, deliverance, healing, or other answers to prayer or active responses from God. Speaking in other tongues has always been an individual experience. Even on the Day of Pentecost, the tongues of fire sat on *each* of them.

Much of today's worship is done in groups. Crowd participation is encouraged by worship teams, and even at the altar someone leads the worship while the people participate together. There is nothing wrong with this practice in itself, unless it limits or stifles individual responses to God. People often stand together at the altar in today's worship, but let us not lose the practice of kneeling at the altar in individual prayer. Each Spirit-filled Christian is both the temple of the Holy Spirit (1 Corinthians 6:19) and a priest unto God (Revelation 1:6).

Spirit-filled people love to go to church, and most attend at least three times a week—Sunday morning, Sunday night, and one or more services or prayer meetings during the week. The New Testament says, "Not forsaking the assembling of ourselves together, as the manner of some is; but exhorting one another: and so much the more, as ye see the day approaching" (Hebrews 10:25). That is, the nearer we are to the second coming of Christ the more we should be in church. Group worship is very important to Pentecostal Christians. Yet, within the context of group participation we must make personal commitments and individual responses to the Lord. In a revived Pentecostal church there will be a strong emphasis on personal spiritual experience.

A study of praise and worship in the Bible yields some surprising results. First, far from being synonymous, "praise" and "worship" have very different meanings and purposes. Second, a number of different Hebrew and Greek words are translated "praise" or "worship." And, third, all the related words in the original languages indicate a commitment to physical and often vocal praise. There can be no question about it—the Pentecostal style of open worship is right!

First, let's look at praise. Seven different Hebrew words are translated "praise" in the King James Version of the Old Testament. *Yâdâh* meant "to hold out the hands, as in worship"; *hillûwi* was "to celebrate or rejoice"; *tehillâh* was "a hymn or vocal praise"; *hâlal* was "to be clean (of color), to shine"; *zâmar* was "to strike with the fingers, as in playing an instrument"; *shâbach* meant "to glorify"; and *mahalâl* (a variation of *hâlal*, "to shine") meant "fame" or "praise." Notice how physical and vocal all those words were. Praise was out loud and demonstrative.

In the New Testament Greek, six words were used in reference to some aspect of praise. *Aînos* meant "praise to God," and the verb form "to praise" was *ainéo*. *Épainos* was another variation on the same word. *Dóxa*, from which we get "doxology," was sometimes translated "praise" or "glory." It came from the verb *dokéo*: "to think, seem, or appear." It had to do with the glorious appearance of God. One New Testament word translated "praise" was *humnéō*: "to sing a hymn of praise." Thus in both the Old Testament and the New there was the idea of praising the Lord with music.

We may see, then, that biblical praise was expressive and vocal. Worshipers were to praise God out loud and often in song. Furthermore, they were to do it by a full involvement of lifting the hands to God, kneeling, or even shouting. Biblically, it's all right to get a little carried away with the Lord.

The biblical idea of worship certainly overlaps with that of praise, but it is even more physical. For example, one of the Old Testament words for "worship" is *shâchâh*, which meant "to prostrate oneself before royalty or God, to bow, or fall down flat." Daniel used an Aramaic form in place of the Hebrew (*segîd* from *sâgad*), but it still meant "to prostrate oneself in homage before God."

The principal New Testament word for "worship" was *proskunéō*—"to prostrate oneself and kiss the feet or the ground; to fall down and worship." Another word was *sébomai*, which meant "to show reverence, or worship." The title *sebastós* ("venerable") was used for the Roman emperor. The word *dóxa* ("praise") was sometimes translated "worship."

What we see, then, is that biblical worship was very physical. Pentecostal Christians have been criticized and even ridiculed for their physical, emotional, and vocal manner of worship; and yet, in truth they have been more biblical in their praise and worship than their critics. It is a sad commentary on the human race that people often make fun of anything they do not understand. The more we comprehend what the Bible says about praise and worship, the more acceptable and desirable we will find the things that happen in a Pentecostal altar service.

The Praise-and-Worship Solution

Glen D. Cole, pastor of Capital Christian Center in Sacramento, California, and an executive presbyter of the Assemblies of God, wrote concerning praise and worship:

"Where churches are failing, praise and worship is the solution. Where lives are failing, praise and worship is the solution. This brings a focus on the Lord by everyone present in the service. The moment one person doesn't do what the body is doing, you have potential division, weakening, if not destroying, the opportunity for God to rain down His 'showers of blessing.'

"Psalm 67:3 declares, 'Let the people praise thee, O God; let all the people praise thee.' This translates very easily into

> Let all the young people praise You!
> Let all the senior citizens praise You!
> Let all the children praise You!
> Let all the congregation praise You!

"Could it be that God gave us speaking in tongues so that all could be equal in worship? We all need help. The Holy Spirit wants to aid us in our worship. When the people cease to be spectators and are known as worshipers, revival will flow to the body.

"The Bible suggests many ways to praise the Lord. Notice these references:

1. Singing—'O sing unto the Lord a new song; for he hath done marvelous things' (Psalm 98:1).
2. Dancing before the Lord—'Thou hast turned for me my mourning into dancing: thou hast put off my sackcloth, and girded me with gladness' (Psalm 30:11).
3. Bowing and kneeling—'O come, let us worship and bow down: let us kneel before the Lord our maker' (Psalm 95:6).
4. Raising our hands—'Thus will I bless thee while I live: I will lift up my hands in thy name' (Psalm 63:4).

5. Clapping our hands—'O clap your hands, all ye people; shout unto God with the voice of triumph' (Psalm 47:1).
6. Praising the Lord with instruments—'Praise him with the sound of the trumpet: praise him with the psaltery and harp. Praise him with the timbrel and dance: praise him with stringed instruments and organs. Praise him upon the loud cymbals: praise him upon the high sounding cymbals. Let every thing that hath breath praise the Lord' (Psalm 150:3–6).
7. Making a joyful noise—'Make a joyful noise unto the Lord, all the earth: make a loud noise, and rejoice, and sing praise' (Psalm 98:4).
8. Shouting for joy—'Let them ever shout for joy' (Psalm 5:11); 'Shout unto God with the voice of triumph' (Psalm 47:1).
9. Singing in the Spirit—'I will sing with the spirit, and I will sing with the understanding also' (1 Corinthians 14:15).
10. Giving offerings—'Give unto the Lord the glory due unto his name: bring an offering, and come into his courts' (Psalm 96:8); 'Therefore, as ye abound in every thing, in faith, and utterance, and knowledge, and in all diligence, and in your love to us, see that ye abound in this grace also' (2 Corinthians 8:7).

"The capstone passage is Psalm 34:2–3—'My soul shall make her boast in the Lord: the humble shall hear thereof, and be glad. O magnify the Lord with me, and let us exalt his name together.'

"Some fall at the feet of singers, actors, athletes, famous personalities, or even things. What would happen if every church body would discover the power of falling at the feet of our great God in praise and worship? I believe the result would be revival!"

Too Carried Away?

Dwight L. Moody, in his 1899 sermon "Revivals," said,

I am not so afraid of excitement as some people. The moment there comes a breath of interest, some people cry, "Sensationalism, sensationalism!" But, I tell you what, I would rather have sensation than stagnation any time. There is nothing a seaman fears so much as fog; he does not fear a storm nearly as much. We have too much fog in the church; let us get out of it.

Get any preacher befogged, and he will say, "I cannot draw the crowds, but then, thank God, I am no sensationalist!"

Let him write a book so dry that it will almost catch fire, and no one thinks of reading it. But he thanks God he is not a sensationalist!

Moody went on to say,

There is no excitement or sensationalism in a graveyard—a man lies where they put him; but I think there will be a stir on the resurrection morning. Where there is life, there will always be a commotion.

Of course we understand that there have been excesses, sensationalism, and self-gratification in the name of Pentecostal worship, but such problems are not as serious as coldness, indifference, and boredom. The question is, What are we so ardent about? We must not be excited about excitement but rather passionately and unreservedly in love with Jesus Christ. We must weep at His cross, rejoice in His resurrection, praise Him in His glory, and await with great anticipation His soon return. Whenever we are in a church service dedicated to His worship and we sense something beyond our human senses—an awareness of His holy presence in the room and in our hearts—we cannot help but break into tears and rush to the altar to fall on our knees before Him. To compare this passion to mere excitement is like comparing love to infatuation. We are fascinated with Jesus, head over heels in love with Him, and thrilled beyond words at every experience of realizing that He loves us, too. When He speaks, we hang on every word, and when He touches us, we behave in ways that only the beloved can ever understand. This is what real Pentecostal services are all about.

Pentecostal people have rediscovered the secret of the New Testament church: that true Christianity is experience with God. Other religions are man seeking after God, but real Christianity is God seeking after man. Salvation is an experience with God, as is water baptism, Communion, the baptism in the Holy Spirit, speaking in other tongues, or receiving divine healing or deliverance. He always is near us, speaking to us, touching us; and when we become aware of His presence we may express ourselves out loud, break into emotion-charged praise, or even shout. We may fall on our faces before Him, lift our hands and praise Him, or perhaps even express our feelings with our feet. Then again, there will be some services when a holy hush falls over the congregation, or weeping, or laughing. In the early days of the Pentecostal movement the people would become so excited that they couldn't stand still, so they would do a "Jericho March" around the inside of the church while shouting the praises of God. No two services were alike, for the mix of people and their expectations always changed and the Lord seldom repeats himself. Pentecostals have always been at their best when they have responded spontaneously to God and at their worst when they have tried to reproduce spiritual phenomena by their own efforts.

Of this we can assure you: When the new revival comes, it will be accompanied by a great amount of enthusiasm and unbridled emotion. When the water is cold, there is little action in the pot, but when you turn up the heat, the water will begin to bubble and boil. Those same believers who respond with feeling in church will carry their faith into the streets and neighborhoods and bring new converts to Christ. Young people moved by God in fervent altar services will be thrust into the ministry to produce our next generation of Pentecostal pastors and missionaries. The fire of the altar will spread out of our controlled fireplaces and set the whole woods aflame!

Will every church be like this? Let us not try to decide in advance what our responses will be. Each church has its own personality and particular combination of people and pastor. But let us not be so determined not to do certain things or express ourselves in certain ways that we miss God. The final proof of revival is not how loud we shout or how many tears we shed, but how many lost souls are brought into the kingdom of God. Church growth in itself is not a sign of revival, but new converts being transformed by the power of Jesus Christ and filled with the Holy Spirit is!

11

Thus Saith the Lord

Thomas Trask and I first began to talk about this book after his election but before his installation as general superintendent of the Assemblies of God. He was, as he is and will be, a man possessed by a purpose. I grew up among people who talked about revival, but I could hardly believe my ears as I heard it expressed so clearly from the new leader of our Fellowship. His eyes would light up as he spoke of revival, and he would often reach for his Bible to support his convictions.

Over the months, as he took office and began his revival campaign, he never swerved from his original mission. The chapel services at our national headquarters began to go beyond their usual half hour, employees responded to altar calls, and national officers anointed the sick with oil. The revival has already begun . . . in Springfield, Missouri!

As our talks continued, Brother Trask often would open his Bible to Jeremiah and read such lines as, "Then the word of the Lord came unto me, saying . . . " (Jeremiah 1:4). I made a note to include a chapter called "Thus Saith the Lord," and suggested he should write it. Most of this book has come out of our conversations together, but this chapter comes directly from the heart of our general superintendent. Here is how the word of the Lord came to him concerning revival in the Assemblies of God. I can see him now as he reached for his Bible and turned to the Book of Jeremiah. . . .

—DAW

In His message to the people of Israel through the prophet Jeremiah, God dealt with the backsliding of His people and identified it as spiritual adultery. In Matthew 19:7–8, Jesus was asked, "Why did Moses then command to give a writing of divorcement, and to put her away?" Our Lord replied, "Moses because of the hardness of your hearts suffered you to put away your wives: but from the beginning it was not so." The hardness of the heart is what leads to spiritual adultery.

God raised up Jeremiah to call Israel to return to Him, and in chapter 3 of his book the prophet repeated the key words again and again—"turn" and "return." The people had left God, but God had not left them.

The first result of Israel's spiritual adultery was that all the land had become polluted. They lived in wickedness and vileness. It is the same picture in our land today. When we depart from spiritual values and forsake God, we become vile and determined to go our own way. Jeremiah 3:2 says, "Thou hast polluted the land with thy whoredoms and with thy wickedness." That was God's rebuke through the prophet.

In Jeremiah 3:1, God had said, "If a man put away his wife, and she go from him, and become another man's, shall he return unto her again? shall not that land be greatly polluted? but thou hast played the harlot with many lovers." This God spoke to Israel's spiritual adultery. The people had forsaken Him, and yet He pleaded, "Return again to me."

The second result of Israel's adultery was that the rains were withheld. Verse 3 says, "Therefore the showers have been withholden, and there hath been no latter rain; and thou hadst a whore's forehead, thou refusedst to be ashamed." What a strong indictment! Where people forsake God, there will be no latter rain. The soul becomes dry, and the spiritual man becomes dead. The dryness of Israel came as a result of indifference, carelessness, callousness, and a lack of responsiveness to the wooing, pleading voice of God. We must be very careful in the church today that we do not become so dry and calloused that the showers of blessing are withheld from us. God cannot and will not bless that which is not clean and pure, not righteous or holy. Only as a holy people can we expect God's blessing.

The third result of Israel's spiritual condition was stubbornness. We find that in verse 3—"Thou hadst a whore's forehead." The Scripture says, "Rebellion is as the sin of witchcraft, and stubbornness is as iniquity and idolatry" (1 Samuel 15:23). That is a powerful statement! Someone might say, "I'm going to do it my way. It's my life, and I can do as I want with it." But we have been married to Jesus, have been bought with a price, and belong to Him.

The fourth result is found in the latter part of Jeremiah 3:3—"Thou refusedst to be ashamed." The people of the world today blatantly live without shame, parading their whoredoms and sins openly and unashamedly. It is a stench in the nostrils of God, and He cannot and will not tolerate it. The church dares not go to bed with the world, for believers must be a separated, peculiar people. Yet, in many cases we have brought the world's music into the church. We have brought the dancing of the world into the church. The theater of the world is condoned as we go to see its productions, and we promote the ungodly lifestyle of those who make the motion pictures and videos. God is not pleased with such behavior!

The people of Israel found themselves living under the awfulness of their sin, and yet God in His providence called His people back to himself. In verse 4, He said, "Wilt thou not from this time cry unto me, My father, thou art the guide of my youth?" We still need to accept Him as Father and Guide. The Scripture describes those "having a form of godliness, but denying the power thereof" (2 Timothy 3:5). People are living unashamedly and become critical of anyone who endeavors to live clean, pure, and holy before God.

In Jeremiah 3:6, the Lord asked Jeremiah, "Hast thou seen that which backsliding Israel hath done? she is gone up upon every high mountain and under every green tree, and there hath played the harlot." The people were offering sacrifices, burning incense, and worshiping the creature more than the Creator. They had rejected the Lord as their lover!

In verse 7, we hear the heart of God, crying, "And I said after she had done all these things"—God in His love, mercy, tenderness, long-suffering, kindness, and wooing calls the church today as He did Israel, saying—"Turn thou unto me." Tragically, the verse continues: "But she returned not."

To the south of Israel was her "treacherous sister Judah" (3:8). In verses 10 through 12, Jeremiah wrote, "And yet for all this her treacherous sister Judah hath not turned unto me with her whole heart, but feignedly, saith the Lord. And the Lord said unto me, The backsliding Israel hath justified herself more than treacherous Judah. Go and proclaim these words toward the north, and say, Return, thou backsliding Israel, saith the Lord; and I will not cause mine anger to fall upon you: for I am merciful, saith the Lord, and I will not keep anger for ever." What a promise! In spite of our backsliding, failure, waywardness, and having grown cold, the Spirit of God still woos the church today.

I plead with the church today, for it is time for us to return to God with all our heart. It wasn't just the fact that Israel was living in shame but that Judah saw it. Jeremiah 3:8 says, "And I saw, when for all the causes whereby backsliding Israel committed adultery, I had put her away, and given her a bill of divorce; yet her treacherous sister Judah feared not, but went and played the harlot also." When the sins of the world begin to penetrate and infiltrate the church, they have a powerfully negative effect. We do not live unto ourselves. Sin will affect the youth, the children, the homes, and the church as a whole. God help us to recognize that the Spirit of the Lord is dealing with the church again. He will not tolerate spiritual adultery but calls to us to return to Him.

God's Processes

Having rebuked backslidden Israel and Judah, God through Jeremiah then begins to speak of a series of processes that could bring them back into His favor. He first makes some divine promises.

In Jeremiah 3:12, God said, "Go and proclaim these words toward the north, and say, Return, thou backsliding Israel, saith the Lord; and I will not cause mine anger to fall upon you." God's first promise was that His anger will be removed if we repent and return to Him. Hebrews 10:31 says, "It is a fearful thing to fall into the hands of the living God." We must recognize again that God is righteous and will judge unrighteousness and sin, whether it be in the church or in the world. Sin is sin and must be dealt with!

God's second promise concerning this restoration is in Jeremiah 3:14, where He said, "Turn, O backsliding children, saith the Lord; for I am married unto you . . . and I will bring you to Zion." If we return to God, His anger will be removed and

He will bring us to Zion. That's the place of victory, joy, beauty, and glory!

His third promise is in verse 15—"I will give you pastors according to mine heart, which shall feed you with knowledge and understanding." We must have pastors in the Assemblies of God who have a heart after God, a heart soft toward God, a heart that hears the voice of God, a heart for the people of God. We need a shepherd's heart, one that is full of knowledge of God and being fed with the manna from on high—the Word of God.

God gave a fourth promise in verse 18—"In those days the house of Judah shall walk with the house of Israel, and they shall come together out of the land of the north to the land that I have given for an inheritance unto your fathers." They would walk together. The Word of God asks, "Can two walk together, except they be agreed?" (Amos 3:3). In Jeremiah 3:14, He said, "I am married unto you." God never intended for a spiritual adultery or a spiritual divorce to take place. He saved us and bought us through the blood of Jesus Christ, and He is able to keep us. "Now unto him that is able to keep you from falling, and to present you faultless before the presence of his glory with exceeding joy, to the only wise God our Saviour, be glory and majesty, dominion and power, both now and ever. Amen" (Jude 24–25). That is the promise of God, but He intended for us to walk together in agreement. Out of that agreement there is power and strength, for "if two of you shall agree on earth as touching any thing that they shall ask, it shall be done for them of my Father" (Matthew 18:19).

He gave yet another promise in Jeremiah 3:18. He would bring them again to the land He had "given for an inheritance." God has an inheritance for His people, the church, but we are living far below God's standards and our privileges in Him. It isn't God's fault! Spiritual adultery, coldness, and indifference come as a result of our backsliding. If we will return, God will keep His promises.

There is a further promise in verse 22—"Return, ye backsliding children, and I will heal your backslidings." And Jeremiah responded, "Behold, we come unto thee; for thou art the Lord our God." Our Lord is not a God of condemnation but of healing and restoration, of returning, help, and strength. The critical issue is whether we will let Him help us return to Him. The prophet Jeremiah could respond with what was in his heart, but would the people follow?

We have been looking at the condition of the people of Israel—backslidden, worshiping gods of stone and wood, and far from God. Yet, the Lord did not give up on them! There are those who feel that the best days of the church are over, but that is not the case—He is our God of restoration. He has the ability to woo us and call us back to himself. Jeremiah 3:12 says, "For I am merciful, saith the Lord." He said through the same prophet in Lamentations 3:22–23, "It is of the Lord's mercies that we are not consumed, because his compassions fail not. They are new every morning."

In Jeremiah 3:14, God said, "I am married unto you." And in verse 22, He said, "Return, ye backsliding children, and I will heal your backslidings." Then in 4:2, Jeremiah affirmed, "The Lord liveth, in truth, in judgment, and in righteousness; and the nations shall bless themselves in him, and in him shall they glory." The devil will do everything in his power to keep us from acknowledging our sin. We must not listen to the enemy because he will destroy. Rather, we must listen to the voice of the Holy Spirit and acknowledge our sinfulness and failure before Him. Jeremiah 17:10 says, "I the Lord search the heart."

The Humbling Process

The first step in our restoration is the humbling process of dealing with our pride. Jeremiah 13:15 says, "Hear ye, and give ear; be not proud: for the Lord hath spoken." God said in 2 Chronicles 7:14, "If my people, which are called by my name [that is, who are married to Me], shall humble themselves, and pray, and seek my face, and turn from their wicked ways"—If we meet His required conditions, He offers His promises—"then will I hear from heaven, and will forgive their sin, and will heal their land." The church cannot make any move toward God without God moving toward us. He is desirous of and is responsive to that relationship.

Both James 4:6 and 1 Peter 5:5 say that God resists the proud but gives grace to the humble. Proverbs 28:13 says, "He that covereth his sins shall not prosper: but whoso confesseth and forsaketh them shall have mercy." The Scripture says, "If we confess our sins, he is faithful and just to forgive us our sins, and to cleanse us from all unrighteousness" (1 John 1:9). The first thing God requires of us in this restoration process is that we acknowledge and recognize that we have fallen short. We must acknowledge that we have left our first love and have failed God miserably.

The Confession Process

The second step is to confess our sins. Confession is the beginning of the cleansing process, for sin is rebellion against the laws of God. We once lived with a sensitivity to the voice of God's Spirit, and our hearts were attuned to Him, but through backsliding our ears became dull and our eyes clouded.

When the Prodigal Son returned home, he said, "Father, I have sinned against heaven, and before thee" (Luke 15:18). That must be the posture of the church today—"Father, we have sinned!" James 5:16 says, "Confess your faults one to another, and pray one for another, that ye may be healed." We must be willing to confess our faults, our transgressions, our sins. Jeremiah 6:26 states, "Gird thee with sackcloth, and wallow thyself in ashes." We must humble ourselves before God and acknowledge that we need the help of the Lord.

In Joshua 7:20, Achan confessed to Joshua, "Indeed I have sinned against the Lord God of Israel." In 1 Samuel 15:24, Saul admitted to Samuel, "I have sinned: for I have transgressed the commandment of the Lord." There will never be any restoration until we first acknowledge our sin and ask God to forgive us. In 2 Samuel 12:13, David confessed to the prophet Nathan, "I have sinned against the Lord." In Mark 1:5, the people of Jerusalem and surrounding Judea went to John the Baptist and "were all baptized of him in the river of Jordan, confessing their sins." Confessing is the beginning of the cleansing process of the heart and soul.

In Jeremiah 15:5–6, God said, "For who shall have pity upon thee, O Jerusalem? or who shall bemoan thee? or who shall go aside to ask how thou doest? Thou hast forsaken me, saith the Lord, thou art gone backward: therefore will I stretch out my hand against thee, and destroy thee; I am weary with repenting."

Confession is acknowledging our sins. That acknowledging begins the process of cleansing. But there are those who will confess only when they have been caught in their sin. Confession is something one does as a result of conviction of the Holy Spirit. The Holy Spirit is faithful to convict, for He will "reprove the world of sin, and of righteousness, and of judgment" (John 16:8). Confession is the result of the heart being touched by God. Such cleansing is a marvelous spiritual experience. The conscience becomes clean, the soul becomes clean, and the mind becomes clean. We take new paths.

Repentance is the demonstration of the sorrow for sin which results in turning away from sin. True repentance is the forsaking of sin. God said to His people, "I am weary with repenting" (Jeremiah 15:6), because they were repenting without forsaking their sins. It is not enough to be sorry for sin because we have gotten caught; we must want to turn away from sin. Israel would repent while the pressure was on, but as soon as it was relieved they would go back to their old ways. They were not sorry for the sin itself.

Paul wrote in 2 Corinthians 7:10, "For godly sorrow worketh repentance to salvation not to be repented of: but the sorrow of the world worketh death." There is a sorrow that works repentance to salvation and cleansing. That is what God wants, for repentance will result in turning from sin. Jesus said to a man whom He had healed, "Thou art made whole: sin no more, lest a worse thing come upon thee" (John 5:14). In John 8:11, Jesus said to a woman taken in adultery, "Neither do I condemn thee: go, and sin no more." God wants repentance that results in a permanent change of our behavior.

The Scripture teaches, "If any man be in Christ, he is a new creature: old things are passed away; behold, all things are become new" (2 Corinthians 5:17). The things we once hated we now love, and the things we once loved we now hate. There is a radical change when we become a new creature in Christ.

The failure to repent of our sins brings serious consequences. Proverbs 29:1 says, "He, that being often reproved hardeneth his neck, shall suddenly be destroyed, and that without remedy." God said to Israel, "I am weary with repenting," because it was meaningless. There had not been a change; confession had become only a religious ritual. We dare not allow that to happen, for confession means nothing without repentance. Paul wrote in Galatians 2:21, "I do not frustrate the grace of God." That is, having been once delivered, he did not live in sin any longer. After Peter had denied the Lord, he "went out, and wept bitterly" (Luke 22:62). That was godly sorrow. The fact is that he did not go back and walk that way again but lived right and clean. That is true repentance! In contrast, Judas' repentance was not a sorrow for his sin to the point of forsaking it, and he ended up taking his own life (Matthew 27:3–5).

The Restoration Process

The pathway to restoration and revival is marked by submission, surrender, and obedience. We must remember these, for God taught them to the prophet with an object lesson about the potter's wheel in Jeremiah 18.

Verses 3 and 4 are key verses, with six words I want to draw attention to: "He," "work," "wheels," "vessel," "marred," and "good." The first one is "He." God is the One who has us under construction. It is God who is dealing with us. It is He who has in His mind what He wants us to be, what the piece of clay should become on the potter's wheel. The potter has a mind picture, a design, of what he is wanting to make. God knows what He wants us to be, so we must be in subjection and submission to His hands, surrendering to Him. Remember, nothing in the clay of itself could make a beautiful vessel. You can entrust that clay to His hands, for He is the Master Potter. For a marvelous testimony, look at the apostle Paul, who said, "For it is God which worketh in you both to will and to do of His good pleasure" (Philippians 2:13).

The second word is "work." There is nothing hit-or-miss about God's program. He is willing to invest His time, energy, love, patience, power, and resources. In Genesis 1:26, God said, "Let us make man in our image," and He made man. He rested on the seventh day from all of His work (Genesis 2:2), but the Holy Spirit continues His work. His finger is upon our lives, working in us, through us, upon us, and upon His church to accomplish His good pleasure. He knows the design of what can become a thing of beauty.

The third word is "wheels." This represents the happenings in life, experiences God uses to shape us. In Philippians 1:12, Paul gave us a good word of admonition that we would do well to follow—"But I would ye should understand, brethren, that the things which happened unto me have fallen out rather unto the furtherance of the gospel." Remember, the wheels of life, the experiences, can either make us or destroy us. "All things work together for good to them that love God, to them who are the called according to his purpose" (Romans 8:28). God intends our experiences to be good and to work for His kingdom's sake.

The fourth word is "vessel," the container. That's what God is making, a vessel of honor. We sometimes sing "A Vessel of Honor for You, Lord." He has to put precious things into His vessels. He has bought us, not with silver and gold but with the precious blood of Jesus Christ. That vessel has to be good. Jesus spoke of not putting new wine into old wineskins. God doesn't use old vessels; He makes new ones, ones that have to be able to hold and display their contents. That is the work of the Spirit, to display the work of God and the presence of Jesus. We are on display. One doesn't take a $6-million Rembrandt and put it out in the toolshed. People build magnificent museums to house such paintings so that people can see them. Well, God is building a magnificent vessel to contain this priceless treasure, but for the present "we have this treasure in earthen vessels" (2 Corinthians 4:7).

The fifth word is "marred," which represents our insisting on having our own way. There is a sovereignty in God that we don't understand. You and I have been given a free moral will, but sin mars a vessel. The Lord is always dealing with marred vessels. You would think He would become tired of it, but He is patient and long-suffering.

According to Jeremiah 18, the purpose of the circumstances of life is that, like the potter's vessel, we can turn out right—"as seemed good to the potter" (verse 4). We must remain soft, pliable, in the hands of the Potter.

In Jeremiah 19, we find that the vessel had become hardened, no longer pliable, no longer moldable, no longer shapable. The Word says it had to be broken. That is a painful process, but if we will stay broken before God, the Scripture says, "A broken spirit . . . and a contrite heart, O God, thou wilt not despise" (Psalm 51:17).

The sixth word is "good." The purposes of God are to bring good, if we will allow Him the privilege of remaking us. God is not in the business of producing junk! He wants good to come from our lives and has the ability to bring good from brokenness, from marred vessels. It behooves us to give God a chance to produce good vessels, both individually and as a church.

I want us to look at this matter of revival and renewal. Revival happens in our hearts and affects the way we live. The result of this is marvelous to behold, for we become people of covenant, people of the promises of God. In this renewal process, the church of Jesus Christ begins to live under God's covenants, or promises, and we become the benefactors. God made a covenant with Israel, saying they would be His people and He would be their God. God has kept His covenant!

In Hebrews 8:6, we learn that Jesus has introduced a better covenant. We must understand the heart of God as it pertains to His promises; He wants to keep His covenant. Psalm 103:17–18 says, "But the mercy of the Lord is from everlasting to everlasting upon them that fear him, and his righteousness unto children's children; to such as keep his covenant, and to those that remember his commandments to do them." Again, in Psalm 105:8–10, we read, "He hath remembered his covenant for ever, the word which he commanded to a thousand generations. Which covenant he made with Abraham, and his oath unto Isaac; and confirmed the same unto Jacob for a law, and to Israel for an everlasting covenant."

In Jeremiah 29:11, God shared His thoughts of peace toward them—"For I know the thoughts that I think toward you, saith the Lord, thoughts of peace, and not of evil, to give you an expected end." Jesus said the same in John 14:27—"Peace I leave with you, my peace I give unto you: not as the world giveth, give I unto you. Let not your heart be troubled, neither let it be afraid."

God is not against the church; He wants it to prosper and enjoy His blessing. He wants to restore the joy of salvation to the church and to answer our prayers. In Jeremiah 29:12, He said, "Then shall ye call upon me, and ye shall go and pray unto me, and I will hearken unto you." If we live in obedience to His ways, He will hear and answer prayer. Jesus said in Matthew 7:11, "If ye then, being evil, know how to give good gifts unto your children, how much more shall your Father which is in heaven give good things to them that ask him?" That's prayer! That's petition!

God wants to keep His covenant with His church. He wants to bless the church and for the church to live under His watchful provision and enjoy His full blessing. But it has to be done God's way. It is God's desire to give back what the devil has stolen from you. In Joel 2:25, He said, "I will restore to you the years that the locust hath eaten, the cankerworm, and the caterpillar, and the palmerworm. . . ." He is a God of restoration and will fulfill His promises.

Jeremiah 29:13 states, "And ye shall seek me, and find me, when ye shall search for me with all your heart." He is found of them that will seek after Him. James 4:8 says, "Draw nigh to God, and he will draw nigh to you." It is not a matter of whether God is looking for us but whether we are looking for God! He is to be found of them that seek Him. That is another marvelous promise! God is accessible; He is available. In Jeremiah 29:14, He said, "I will be found of you, saith the Lord: and I will turn away your captivity, and I will gather you from all the nations, and from all the places whither I have driven you, saith the Lord; and I will bring you again into the place whence I caused you to be carried away captive." Mankind is being held hostage by the enemy, but God is able to rescue. He said, "I will [cause] you to return" (verse 10).

In Jeremiah 30, God gave us a further promise of this restoration process and the work of the Holy Spirit in our lives. In verse 17, He said, "I will restore health unto thee, and I will heal thee of thy wounds, saith the Lord." There needs to be a river of God open to the church of Jesus Christ today. There needs to be healing, for healing is in the covenant. In Exodus 15:26, He said, "I am the Lord that healeth thee." Certainly He has the ability and wants to accomplish that in our lives.

In Jeremiah 30, He gave us some further benefits and promises. Verse 19 says, "And out of them shall proceed thanksgiving and the voice of them that make merry: and I will multiply them, and they shall not be few; I will also glorify them, and they shall not be small." He said that instead of grumbling and complaining there would be thanksgiving and rejoicing with praise. The Word of God instructs us, "With joy shall ye draw waters out of the wells of salvation" (Isaiah 12:3). Instead of diminishing, He said a multiplication will take place. God has the ability to multiply as Jesus multiplied the loaves and the fishes. The church is meant to become bigger in spirit, bigger numerically, bigger in the things of God. He said that instead of being ashamed and a reproach, we will be glorified and honored.

It is not God's plan for the church to live in shame and reproach. That is not the Master Potter's design for the clay. His plan is that the church should bring glory and honor unto Him.

In Jeremiah 30:20, God said, "Their children also shall be as aforetime, and their congregation shall be established before me, and I will punish all that oppress them." It is God's plan that our children should serve Him and walk in the beauty of holiness. He said He would defeat the enemy and punish them that oppress.

In Jeremiah 17:7, He said, "Blessed is the man that trusteth in the Lord, and whose hope the Lord is. For he shall be as a tree planted by the waters, and that spreadeth out her roots by the river, and shall not see when heat cometh, but her leaf shall be green; and shall not be careful in the year of drought, neither shall cease from yielding fruit." Again, we are covenant people, and revival brings renewal to our hearts.

The Building Process

In this restoration, or revival, there are additional ingredients in this new covenant that we discover in Jeremiah 31. When Jesus said He would build His church and the gates of hell would not prevail against it (Matthew 16:18), that was no idle promise. In Jeremiah 31:4, the Lord said, "Again I will build thee, and thou shalt be built, O virgin of Israel: thou shalt again be adorned with thy tabrets, and shalt go forth in the dances of them that make merry." God is in the construction business, and the devil is in demolition. The devil is out to destroy the church; but God is in the process of building His church, and "the gates of hell shall not prevail against it."

God said He would again adorn His bride. He will again adorn His church with His Spirit, with His robe of righteousness, His peace, His holiness, His character, His likeness, His beauty, and His fragrance. He said, "Thou shalt yet plant vines upon the mountains of Samaria: the planters shall plant, and shall eat them as common things" (31:5). In 31:20, He said of Israel, "I do earnestly remember him still."* God's heart is for His church.

---

*The Book of Jeremiah, which starts out comparing Israel to a woman, does not maintain this same imagery throughout. There is some evidence that the name of Israel for the Northern Kingdom was often considered feminine and the alternate name Ephraim was masculine. Jeremiah 31 has both images in the same chapter.

Jeremiah 31:6 says, "For there shall be a day, that the watchmen upon the mount Ephraim shall cry, Arise ye, and let us go up to Zion unto the Lord our God." There is a cry going out today, a cry from the hearts of people to arise once more and go to Zion. Let us appeal to God, to seek God! Wherever this cry is being heard and men and women are responding, there is a marvelous move of the Spirit of God that is saying, "Let's go back to the house of the Lord!"

Concerning restoration, revival, and renewal, Jeremiah 31:9 says, "They shall come with weeping, and with supplications will I lead them: I will cause them to walk by the rivers of waters in a straight way, wherein they shall not stumble." Oh, what a marvelous promise! In that walk by the rivers of water I see the divine source that comes from God. No wonder the psalmist David said, "Yea, though I walk through the valley of the shadow of death, I will fear no evil: for thou art with me" (Psalm 23:4).

God said, "I am a father to Israel, and Ephraim [another name for Israel] is my firstborn" (Jeremiah 31:9). He is our Father, who watches over us. "If ye then, being evil, know how to give good gifts unto your children: how much more shall your heavenly Father give the Holy Spirit to them that ask him?" (Luke 11:13).

Jeremiah wrote in 31:10, "Hear the word of the Lord, O ye nations, and declare it in the isles afar off, and say, He that scattered Israel will gather him, and keep him, as a shepherd doth his flock." God is for His church and is watching over the sheep of His flock. He said He would gather them, keep them, and care for them.

That's the work of the Holy Spirit! He said in verse 14, "I will satiate the soul of the priests with fatness, and my people shall be satisfied with my goodness." Oh, that's so wonderful! There shall be rejoicing "for wheat, and for wine, and for oil, and for the young of the flock and of the herd: and their soul shall be as a watered garden; and they shall not sorrow any more at all" (31:12). It is the provision of God that we have bountifulness, that we have a supply of the Spirit within our hearts. It is wonderful to behold!

As a result of the restoration of revival, God said in 31:16, "Thus saith the Lord; Refrain thy voice from weeping, and thine eyes from tears: for thy work shall be rewarded, saith the Lord;

and they shall come again from the land of the enemy." He promises that our work will be rewarded. There is hope instead of dismay, faith instead of discouragement and unbelief. "There is hope in thine end, saith the Lord, that thy children shall come again to their own border" (verse 17). There are those today who feel like the condition is hopeless, but there is hope.

Jeremiah declared in 31:19, "Surely after that I was turned, I repented; and after that I was instructed." There is instruction that comes to the church by the voice of the Holy Spirit. He says, "And thine ears shall hear a word behind thee, saying, This is the way, walk ye in it, when ye turn to the right hand, and when ye turn to the left" (Isaiah 30:21).

In Jeremiah 31:22, God said, "How long wilt thou go about, O thou backsliding daughter? for the Lord hath created a new thing in the earth." That's the work of the Holy Spirit. There is a new wind blowing, a wind by the Spirit of God. In verse 25, He said, "For I have satiated the weary soul, and I have replenished every sorrowful soul." That's God's further promise for us.

In chapter 32, we see Jeremiah in the jailhouse when the word of the Lord came to him. Throughout the Book of Jeremiah we find variations of "the word of the Lord came unto Jeremiah" or "thus saith the Lord." There has to be the word of the Lord. God is speaking to us through His Word today, and we must have our ear tuned to what His voice is saying.

Jeremiah's cousin, Hanameel, came to Jeremiah to offer a plot of family ground in Anathoth. He said, "Buy thee my field that is in Anathoth: for the right of redemption is thine to buy it" (verse 7). The right of redemption is ours. It is a right that God has given to us—a right to claim the promises of God and to walk in His provision. That's not presumption; it is a right God has given to His church.

In the providence of that right we will know of God's goodness to us. We live far below our privilege, not because it is God's fault but because we have failed to live in the provision God has promised. The Lord would pass through the land, and they were going to be revived and once again experience His blessings.

The Finishing Process

We find our supernatural dwelling place in what Jeremiah wrote in 32:17: "Ah Lord God! behold, thou hast made the heaven and the earth by thy great power and stretched out arm, and there is nothing too hard for thee." That is where the church must live. There is nothing too difficult for the God we serve. Verse 27 declares, "Behold, I am the Lord, the God of all flesh: is there any thing too hard for me?"

May we hear it again—"I am the Lord!" God put His name on the line and stands behind all His promises. In verse 37, He promised, "I will gather them out of all countries," and in verse 38, He said, "They shall be my people, and I will be their God." In verse 39, He stated, "I will give them one heart," and in verse 40, He added, "I will make an everlasting covenant with them, that I will not turn away from them, to do them good." Finally, in verse 41, He promised, "Yea, I will rejoice over them to do them good."

Oh, what an amazing promise God has given to His church today. Let us believe God for this revival, this restoration. Believe with us for this last-day revival that the Holy Spirit of God is bringing to the Assemblies of God. I want you to look up in faith. I want you to believe. He is the Lord God Omnipotent who reigns forever. Praise be to God!

12

Where Revival Begins

The story of Samson is deeply disturbing for anyone sincerely concerned about revival. It is too much like looking into a mirror and seeing our own faults.

At first Samson was the hope of the nation of Israel, representing a revival of operating in the power of the Spirit of God rather than in the strength of men. Yet, Samson relied on his physical signs of holiness to carry him through rather than establishing any real depth of relationship with God, and he suffered from a human malady: he could not keep his eyes off the world. He considered his miraculous exploits proofs of God's blessing; even as he was lying in the arms of the wicked Delilah he failed to see his own downfall approaching. Before he realized it, he had been shorn of his power and reduced to bondage.

It is enlightening to note that Samson did not once speak of God until after his undoing. Yet, between Judges 13:24 and 16:20 he said "I," "me," "my," "mine," or "myself" thirty-seven times. In his beginning, "the child grew, and the Lord blessed him" (13:24), but by the time Delilah was through with him, "he wist not that the Lord was departed from him" (16:20). He trusted in physical aspects of holiness and yet played with immorality and temptation as if they would have no effect on him. He was publicly opposed to the world, while privately he was drawn to the "woman of Timnath of the daughters of the Philistines" (14:1), the "harlot" of Gaza (16:1), and "a woman in the valley of Sorek, whose name was Delilah" (16:4–20).

Self-indulgence and self-denial are opposites, and each cancels out the other. We cannot do exploits in the name of the Lord and at the same time dally with Delilah! The world may not at first know of our sin, but it will witness our ineffectiveness where once we slew the lions and set the fields aflame.

From his own viewpoint, Samson was pleased with himself and finding pleasure with Delilah at the very moment that he was being stripped of his power. He did not even know that "the Lord was departed from him" (16:20). It was only in his dying moments that "Samson called unto the Lord, and said, O Lord God, remember me, I pray thee, and strengthen me, I pray thee, only this once, O God" (16:28). Even then, his motivation was not to work for God but to avenge himself—"that I may be at once avenged of the Philistines for my two eyes." Yes, God did revive him and gave him one more victory, but how much better it would have been if Samson had never sinned! If he had kept his eyes on God rather than Delilah, he never would have lost them. A loss of vision is one of the tragic results when those who are called to holiness and to do exploits for God fall into the hands of an immoral world.

So here we are at the threshold of a new century and a new millennium with our vision fading and our strength ebbing. We have known both holiness and the power of God, and yet have played with the world. Now once more we are crying out, "Lord, bless us one more time." If God is going to give us another revival, we're going to have to get our morality right, our holiness right, and stop seeing the world as the source of our pleasure.

What Exactly Are We Looking For?

It would be a grave error for us to predetermine what God is about to do. In fact, our revival must begin with a fresh reliance upon God and His will rather than upon our own talents, money, or power. We are apt to look to our slower growth and generally less effective methods as the source of our problems and think that if we will just stir ourselves up we will soon have everything rolling forward again. However, God looks on the heart and sees our spiritual shallowness.

For a biblical example of a shallow approach to revival, we may turn to Hosea 6:1–3, which says, "Come, and let us return unto the Lord: for he hath torn, and he will heal us; he hath smitten, and he will bind us up. After two days will he revive us: in the third day he will raise us up, and we shall live in his sight. Then shall we know, if we follow on to know the Lord: his going forth is prepared as the morning; and he shall come unto us as the rain, as the latter and former rain unto the earth."

Most ministers have preached from that passage, for it contains wonderful phrases about returning to the Lord, being healed, and being revived. The problem is that we expect it all in a three-day revival campaign!

Have we failed to read the rest of the passage? God is not pleased with our shallow revivals. In verse 4, He asks, "What shall I do unto thee? For your goodness is as a morning cloud, and as the early dew it goeth away." Three-day revivals will not revive us! Our spirituality comes and quickly goes like the morning dew. Our attitude of alternating between momentary revival rains and long periods of dryness is insincere and causes God's anger rather than His pleasure. Therefore, God has hewn His people with His prophets, slain them by the words of His mouth, and sent His judgment like the rising of the sun (verse 5).

So, what does God want us to do? He told us clearly through the prophet Hosea: "For I desired mercy, and not sacrifice; and the knowledge of God more than burnt offerings" (verse 6). That is, a true revival will not be temporary, like the morning dew that burns off as soon as the hot sun strikes it, but will produce lasting changes in our behavior. God wants "mercy" (right attitudes toward others) and "knowledge of God" (truly knowing and loving Him) rather than going through the motions of religious traditions and periodic revivals. The awakening we seek must be a restoration of a burden for the needs of others and an insatiable hunger for knowing God.

If we are physically alive, we can open our eyes and see the material world around us; and when we are spiritually alive we become aware of what is happening in the realm of the Spirit. Recognizing that God is actively present in a church service, Spirit-filled people have an intense expectancy that something supernatural, something spiritual, is about to happen. This explains our enthusiasm, our open praise, and our trust in God for miracles of salvation, deliverance, healing, and power.

We have so overused the word *revival* and have for so long

applied it to series of meetings that we have about forgotten any long-term meaning. We have revived ourselves many times and gotten a few weeks of enthusiasm before dropping back again into our normal behavior. What we need now is a whole new spiritual awakening for today and for the twenty-first century! We don't need just a momentary jolt from a cup of strong coffee but a deep drink at the fountain of God's blessing.

A Restoration of First Love

As we have seen, the Early Church needed no revival because it was enjoying the blessings of primary experience. Yet, as the generations passed, the first-century church encountered the same problems we face. By the time John wrote the Book of Revelation, all the other disciples were gone, and few Christians in the churches knew anybody who had seen Jesus. That's our biggest problem: With passing generations we lose sight of our original experience and purpose.

Our best insight into this problem comes from Revelation 2:4, where about A.D. 95 the Lord said to the church in Ephesus, "Nevertheless I have somewhat against thee, because thou hast left thy first love." What a sad commentary on a church that had started out with speaking in tongues and miracles and had spread the gospel all over Asia Minor (Acts 19:10)!

First love speaks to us of courtship, when that special girl or boy was the focal point of all our attention, the most important person in the whole world. Yet, as the saying goes, familiarity breeds contempt. Even with a beautiful and loving husband or wife, we get used to our blessings and settle into the routines of life. American journalist Helen Rowland said, "When a girl marries she exchanges the attentions of many men for the inattention of one."

Something similar happens with Christians. We can hear the story of the Cross so often that we become jaded, no longer moved at our Lord's suffering. We become dispassionate about His passion! We can grow so accustomed to the supernatural that we lose the state of expectancy needed for anything supernatural to occur.

The Lord offered the solution to Ephesus' decline. He said, "Remember therefore from whence thou art fallen, and repent, and do the first works; or else I will come unto thee quickly, and will remove thy candlestick out of his place, except thou repent" (Revelation 2:5). To be revived, the Ephesian church was required to *remember, repent,* and *return.* The same cure will work for us today. We must recall the spiritual heights where we once climbed, repent of our loss of intensity, and regain what we once had. The Lord is not pleased with our present condition, for He says, "I have somewhat against thee."

What Will It Take to Restore Us?

Donald G. Bloesch, in *The Crisis of Piety,* said,

> What is needed today is a renewal of devotion to the living Saviour, Jesus Christ. Such renewal will take the form of a spiritual reformation that involves the very structure and life of the church. . . . Yet it is to be recognized that authentic renewal finally rests upon a new outpouring of the Holy Spirit. Indeed it is only the Spirit that enables us to pray and to preach with power and conviction. It is the Spirit who empowers us for service in the kingdom of God. It is the Spirit who pours meaning into the language of faith and who enlightens those to whom this language is addressed. The renewal of devotion in our time will entail a rediscovery of the role of the Holy Spirit in Christian faith and practice.

The path to spiritual awakening leads through a renewal of devotion, prayer, Christian meditation (thinking on God and His Word), and faith to the exclusion of worldly interests. A sharpness of spiritual focus is required at the expense of throwing everything else out of focus until the very world begins to blur before our eyes.

The problem with a spiritual awakening is that we don't know how to wake up. We are like the man who dreamed he was asleep, and when in his dream he woke up, he was still sleeping! We cannot awaken ourselves. Somebody has to sound the alarm. God declared through the prophet Joel, "Blow ye the trumpet in Zion, and sound an alarm in my holy mountain" (Joel 2:1). Jeremiah said, "Blow ye the trumpet in the land: cry, gather together, and say, Assemble yourselves" (Jeremiah 4:5).

We have had some great leaders in the past, each with the demands and struggles of his times; but now, to face the challenges of this day, God has brought together a team of men experienced in revival to call this Movement to a new awakening. Two years before his election as general superintendent, Thomas E. Trask wrote in a General Presbytery resolution, "Whereas there is evidence in our Fellowship that God is wanting to kindle the fire of revival, it is imperative that we fan that flame."

General Secretary George O. Wood wrote for this book,

> Looking back at the twentieth century in review, we can see the early rains of Topeka, Kansas; Azusa Street in Los Angeles; Hot Springs, Arkansas. This was the softening of the ground for the planting of the end-time harvest. Now, we are at the conclusion of this century and millennium. I have felt the Holy Spirit saying to me, "Azusa Street was only a shower compared to what I purpose to do in the days yet ahead." The greater harvest is yet to come, and that's why the rain is yet needed.

A Recipe for Revival

For any recipe to work, there must be the right combination of ingredients, temperature, and timing. We believe that those elements are now present in the Assemblies of God and that we are on the verge of a new awakening in our Fellowship.

Is there a recipe for revival? We think so! We cannot get the ingredients merely by studying previous revivals any more than we could get the flour and sugar back from a cake. In fact, the necessary ingredients defy description because the elements of revival are a lot like falling in love.

Assuming that at this point we want to be revived, let us examine the necessary ingredients of a revival recipe.

First, we have to want to be revived. That is, we must be in a state of mind that will allow God to awaken us and renew our spiritual lives. This in itself is not enough because wanting revival is like wanting to be in love. Revival, like love, results from a relationship. Yet there must be a certain predisposition toward revival, a permission in the mind, that allows us to accept revival when it comes.

Second, we must meet the right Person. Revival is not something in the air like some fragrance; it is a highly personal response to our personal Lord, a love relationship with Jesus Christ.

As in love, revival begins and resides in the heart. According to *Power* magazine,

Newspapermen went down from London to report at first hand the marvelous happenings of the great Welsh Revival at the turn of the century. On their arrival in Wales one of them asked a policeman where the Welsh Revival was. Drawing himself to his full height he laid his hand over his heart and proudly proclaimed: "Gentlemen, the Welsh Revival is inside this uniform!"

What we need is not revival for its own sake but a freshly impassioned love for the Lord Jesus Christ—when He is uppermost in our minds, when our hearts leap for joy at His approach and we gladly set aside all other interests just to be with Him and please Him. That is how a revival begins.

Have you ever seen an ugly bride? Never! Not everyone has the privilege of being born beautiful, but let love come into the heart and something wonderful happens. The woman's features change, her very walk is different, and there is a glow to her personality and a light in her eyes that declare to the whole world, "I am in love!" This enamored state reaches a high and intensely emotional pitch in the times surrounding the wedding, but for two people in love it can last for the rest of their lives.

This is what will happen when we fall in love with Jesus. We are His bride, and He is the Groom. The wedding will take place as soon as He returns, and we keep glancing out the window to see if He is coming down the road. He is in love with His church and will soon return "that he might present it to himself a glorious church, not having spot, or wrinkle, or any such thing; but that it should be holy and without blemish" (Ephesians 5:27).

That bright-eyed state of loving expectancy is what we mean by revival. It is the personal transformation, the feeling of being truly alive, that occurs in people in love. Such revived Christians will want to read the Bible and linger on every word as if it were a love letter. They will want to be in church services, joyfully entering into prayer, and sitting on the edge of their seats in anticipation at the preaching of the Word. Furthermore, one can hardly get such Christians to talk about anything else but Jesus. His name comes easily to their lips, and every subject reminds them of something He has said or done. That is revival! You can no more define it than you can explain love, but you can experience it and will know without doubt when you have it.

Our problem is how to attain that high state of revival, that spiritual awakening. No one yet has fallen in love by reading a book on the subject, any more than you will fall into revival by reading this one. There is no easy one, two, three—*revival!* The very best we can do is to introduce you to Jesus. You won't be able to explain it, although you might endlessly try to do so; however, you will look into His eyes, be captivated by His manner of treating you as if you were the only person in the world, and be swept off your feet in love with Him.

This is what the Ephesian Christians had lost. They had left their first love! God's remedy for such a condition is to remember, repent, and return.

Here we reach the very crux of our present need. How may we rekindle our lost love for Jesus? We have said there is no easy formula for revival, but there is a way that is so effective that your own human nature will resist it and all the demons in hell will fight it. It is so simple that every born-again child of God can describe it, and yet few people ever do it. You can find this formula in James 4:7–10—"Submit yourselves therefore to God. Resist the devil, and he will flee from you. Draw nigh to God, and he will draw nigh to you. Cleanse your hands, ye sinners; and purify your hearts, ye double-minded. Be afflicted, and mourn, and weep: let your laughter be turned to mourning, and your joy to heaviness. Humble yourselves in the sight of the Lord, and he shall lift you up."

That's it, the secret of revival!

1. Revival starts with submission to the will and ways of God. You must give yourself permission to be revived and submit yourself to the process. Like falling in love, you choose whether you will submit to it and allow it to continue.

2. When you fall in love, you reject all other lovers. Revival will never come unless you turn your back on the devil and your own sins. You cannot be in love with Jesus and at the same time be enamored of the sins of the world. This involves repentance, which is both a confession of sin and a turning away from sin. Sorrow for sin is not enough; you must reject it. Jesus Christ demands our whole heart, soul, and mind and will accept nothing less than a total commitment to Him.

3. Having turned your heart to God, you must draw nearer to Him. As you do so, He will draw nearer to you. That is when you realize how deeply you have fallen in love. This intimate relationship comes out of (1) reading His Word with sincere interest and devotion, (2) spending quality time in seeking His face in

145

prayer, and (3) entering into worship with a sense of expectancy of His presence and power.

4. As strange as it may seem, falling in love first produces an uneasiness, an awkwardness with oneself at such a change of life-style. There will be little joy at the beginning of revival, for as you approach His perfection you will become aware of your imperfections, your failures, and your own ugliness. You will find you are not dressed for the occasion, and in the purity of His presence you will be embarrassed that your face is dirty, your clothes are wrinkled and soiled, and you are so clumsy that you keep stumbling over your own feet. The fight-or-flight syndrome takes over, and you must either do something about yourself or turn and run away. James tells you to wash your hands, remove all impurities from your heart, repent and weep with sorrow for sin, and grieve over the past wanderings of your wayward life. Then, humble yourself in the sight of the Lord. You have to go back to the fountain of salvation and be cleansed of your sin with the blood of Jesus. As the Lord said to the Ephesians: Remember, repent, and return!

5. As you cleanse yourself and come before Him in the beauty of holiness, revival will come. Sorrow for sin will be replaced with the joy of the Lord, and you will find yourself more and more in love with Jesus. Indeed, "he shall lift you up."

6. You will meet others who have made similar commitments to Christ and will come together to pray for revival. If you are a pastor, you will call your congregation to prayer and fasting. As individuals are awakened, the whole church will come alive. Sinners will be attracted to the services, and as they are converted they will bring great joy and enthusiasm to the church, which in turn will attract even more people.

7. When your church is revived, other people will become aware of God's blessings, other churches will be awakened, and revival will spread like a fire across our land.

There can be no doubt that the coming revival will begin in the hearts of individual Christians who remember, repent, and return to their first love. What a wonderful idea—falling in love again with Jesus! That is exactly how the new revival must begin. In fact, it already has begun in the hearts of praying people all over America, and the world is about to find out about it.

When Will It Happen?

Charles G. Finney, an evangelist greatly used of God in another day, wrote in *Revivals of Religion* that there are eight signs of an approaching revival.

1. When the providence of God indicates that a revival is at hand.

2. When the wickedness of the wicked grieves and humbles and distresses Christians.

3. A revival may be expected when Christians have a spirit of prayer for revival.

4. Another sign that a revival may be expected is when the attention of ministers is especially directed to this particular object, and when their preaching and other efforts are aimed particularly at the conversion of sinners.

5. A revival of religion may be expected when Christians begin to confess their sins to one another.

6. A revival may be expected whenever Christians are found willing to make the sacrifices necessary to carry it on.

7. A revival may be expected when ministers and professors are willing to have God promote it by whatsoever instruments He pleases. Sometimes ministers are not willing to have a revival unless *they* can have the management of it.

8. Strictly, I should say that when the foregoing things occur, a revival, to some extent, already exists. In truth a revival should be *expected* whenever it is *needed*.

Even the greatest of revivals must begin in the hearts of individual Christians. Thomas DeCourcy Rayner wrote,

The world still feels the influence of the great Welsh Revival which flamed across the tiny country of Wales at the beginning of this century. But few remember just how this mighty spiritual movement began:

A Christian Endeavor meeting was in progress in a small town in Wales when a timid young Welsh girl arose. She was so nervous that she could utter only one short sentence: "O, I do love Jesus!" Then she sat down. The Lord used that earnest testimony to fulfill His own divine purposes. Spiritual fire came down on that young people's meeting, even akin to Pentecost. Quickly it spread through that church, then through the little town, and on through the whole of Wales. Its influence was soon felt all around the world.

Oh, God, do it again!

13

A Pentecostal Altar Call

There comes a moment in many Pentecostal services when at the end of the sermon the preacher is apt to say, "Every head bowed, and every eye closed." It is not intended so much for contemplation by the congregation as for some privacy for those who might respond to an invitation to salvation. The practice has served as a courtesy to people making decisions for Christ.

This is our altar call.

This book is a Pentecostal sermon. Under a strong sense of anointing, we have delivered to you the message God has laid on our hearts, and now it is your opportunity to respond to the urging of the Holy Spirit. No book has ever been written like this, but right now the same Holy Spirit, who has been speaking to and through us, is talking to you.

- Do you desire a spiritual awakening in your life and in the Assemblies of God?
- Can we count on you to participate in the coming revival with all your heart, soul, mind, and strength?
- Will you join us in serious prayer, with fasting if the Lord should so direct, until we see a fresh outpouring of the Holy Spirit in America?
- Will you ask the Lord to help you separate yourself from worldliness and live in holiness and righteousness before God?
- Will you work in unity with other Spirit-filled Christians in

your church and become active at the altar and in prayer until the revival comes?

- If you are a pastor, will you draw nearer to God yourself and then lead your congregation into revival by your Pentecostal service style, preaching, altar calls, and evangelism?
- If you are an itinerant evangelist or missionary, will you ask the Lord to so fill you with His Holy Ghost and fire that you will leave a flaming trail of revived churches behind you?
- If you are a teacher, will you enter wholeheartedly into this spiritual awakening yourself and instill the truths of Pentecostal life and doctrine into your students so as to provide the next generation of Spirit-anointed preachers?
- Will you join with us in declaring before God that you will not rest until revival comes?

If your answer is *yes* to the above questions that apply to you, we welcome you to God's new order of "prayer warriors." That's not the name of a program, but we will know one another by the revival fires that spring up around us. God keeps the roll, and He will bless and anoint those who rise up to call for a fresh revival in our land.

Altar calls sometimes fall short of completion because those who respond are not told what to do next. In the following pages we will seek to guide you into becoming the person God wants you to be and into doing what He wants you to do.

Let us first address you individually; for whether you are a layperson or a minister, you must relate personally and intimately to God. Later, we will give direction to ministers. The scope of the coming revival will be broad, but it will be made up of awakened and spiritually aware individuals who love the Lord and long for a fresh outpouring of His Holy Spirit.

Revived Believers

Three Bible passages will lead you as you seek a personal and corporate revival: 2 Chronicles 7:14, James 4:7–10, and Revelation 2:1–5.

The first passage is in the Old Testament: God said, "If my people, which are called by my name, shall humble themselves, and pray, and seek my face, and turn from their wicked ways; then will I hear from heaven, and will forgive their sin, and will heal their land" (2 Chronicles 7:14).

This verse leaves no possibility of doubt about what you are supposed to do. A true revival must begin with self-denial and humility. The Lord must come first in our lives, and all else must be secondary or denied. You will want to stop any worldly practices, and as you put God first, even some things not evil in themselves will become less important. You must exchange your selfishness and pride for selflessness and humility. Jesus said, "If any man will come after me, let him deny himself, and take up his cross, and follow me" (Matthew 16:24).

Having humbled yourself and adopted a holy life-style, you are then in a condition to pray effectively. Prayer is the single most important element in revival. We are not speaking here of short prayers, such as those over food or for opening a church service. Rather, you need quality time with the Lord to shut out the world and become aware of the leading of the Holy Spirit. In 1 Timothy 2:1, the apostle Paul spoke of "supplications [crying out to God, putting emotions behind your prayers], prayers [words to God, talking with Him], intercessions [praying for someone else, praying for revival], and giving of thanks [prayers of praise]." Some say these are different kinds of prayer, but we also may think of them as elements of a single prayer session. Let your emotions flow as you express how you feel about Jesus, then let your thoughts flow as you express what you think to Him. Let these be followed by your compassion, caring and interceding for others, and let your spirit flow in praise to Him. You will find it will be in this latter state of communion with the Lord that you will hear His voice.

The Bible has much to say about fasting and prayer. Many have proclaimed physical health benefits of fasting, but the main purpose is to withdraw from the world so that you might bring the flesh under subjection and give full attention to God. Other kinds of fasts might include radio and television silence as a spiritual discipline.

Next, you are to seek God's face. It is one thing to talk to God and quite another to become aware of His presence. Some believers sense yes-or-no confirmations from the Lord, while others receive words or short phrases. Some have visions, and others do not. We must not judge one another in these matters, for the Lord has different ministries for each of us. However, the more time we spend communicating with the Lord the better we will become at it. Hebrews 5:14 says, "But strong meat belongeth to them that are of full age, even those who by reason of use have their senses exercised to discern both good and evil." As we use our spiritual senses, we get better at communicating with the Lord.

Finally, you must turn from your wicked ways. Today's churchgoer is apt to ask, "What wicked ways?" We have become so accustomed to wickedness that we are no longer shocked or bothered by it. In the early days of television, many Christians would turn off their sets when a beer commercial came into their homes, but today such invasions of our Christian house- holds are ignored or accepted as a normal environment. To be worldly is to act like the world. To our shame, there is little dif- ference today between the Christian life-style and that of the greater society.

How can we claim to be the bride of Christ and yet fill our minds with immoral sex and violence through television, motion pictures, and videos? We contradict ourselves! We teach one thing on Sunday and then turn around and entertain ourselves by watching other people sin. This is not meant to start a "wickedness list," but the closer you get to God the more of the world you will cut out of your life.

If you want to be a prayer warrior for revival, you must hum- ble yourself, pray, seek God's face, and turn from your wicked ways. Then, and only then, will God hear you, forgive your sins, and bring healing to your body, mind, and spirit.

The second passage for you to consider is James 4:7–10, where we are told to submit ourselves to God, resist the devil, draw nigh to God, cleanse our hands, purify our hearts, be afflicted and weep, and humble ourselves. Every phrase in that passage seems to go contrary to the world. There must be a new holiness, based not on yesterday's legalism but on today's power of choice. Jesus said it clearly: "No man can serve two mas- ters: for either he will hate the one, and love the other; or else he will hold to the one, and despise the other. Ye cannot serve God and mammon" (Matthew 6:24). Drawing closer to God implies a moving away from contrary things. John said, "Love not the world, neither the things that are in the world. If any man love the world, the love of the Father is not in him" (1 John 2:15).

The third passage for the reviving Christian is one we explored in the previous chapter—Revelation 2:1–5. There the

Lord through John told us to remember how we used to be, repent of our backsliding, and return to do what we used to do: *Remember, repent,* and *return.*

If you have not been baptized in the Holy Spirit with speaking in other tongues, according to Acts 2:4, make receiving that experience your spiritual priority. Jesus would not let His disciples begin their ministries until they had received what He called "the promise of the Father." Once you have been filled with the Holy Spirit, speak in tongues often in your prayer times. First Corinthians 14:4 says it edifies you, builds you up. Ask the Lord to use you for His service and in the operation of the spiritual gifts (1 Corinthians 12:1–11).

There is much more we could say about individual response to revival, for we are dealing here with the whole range of the Christian life. As revival comes, the Holy Spirit will lead you into all truth (John 16:13).

Revived Ministers

It may seem contradictory to speak of reviving ministers, but many of us feel it is precisely because of an uninspired and uninspiring clergy that we are in our present condition. Many of today's ministers have never witnessed a revival such as the one that is about to spread across our land. They were raised in unrevived churches and never learned how to operate in the Spirit. Others have known revival and yet have failed to understand that it is supposed to be a continuing condition rather than a temporary state of excitement. The 1901 outpouring at Topeka lasted only a short time, and the Azusa Street revival of 1906 was over by 1910; but those revival meetings were only the beginning of a broader and deeper revival movement that affected most of the twentieth century. We are not asking God for a few short years of revival but for a great awakening for the twenty-first century!

Some pastors know what it takes to have a revival but may not be willing to pay the price in commitment, operating in the Spirit, and plain hard work. May God make us a committed clergy, who will do whatever it takes, at whatever price, at whatever hours of the day or night, in the face of whatever opposition—to experience revival in our churches and across our land!

152

All our ministers—pastors, evangelists, teachers, missionaries, musicians, administrators—must plunge wholeheartedly into this revival and lead the people in responding to the Spirit of God. For the sake of brevity, we will address the following pages to pastors because of their essential role in leading our congregations, but our prayer is that every minister will take this admonition to heart and lead the way back to God.

Pastor, can we count on you to commit yourself and your congregation to revival?

First, you must get yourself revived.

Get alone with God! Find a place of solitude, of silencing the sounds of the man-made world. (Brother Trask and I exchanged knowing smiles when we talked about this. When Thomas Trask was a pastor in Detroit, he had a private place where he would get alone to pray. While pastoring in San Jose, California, I found a seacoast cave where the only sounds were those of the sea gulls and the crashing surf. Perhaps if it had not been for what happened in those secret places alone with God we might not be writing to you of these things today.)

You may need to get out of the area of your pastoral duties, outside the zone you feel responsible for—especially if you have sensed the spirit of your area and find you must combat it daily. This is not the time or place to go into any study of demonic activities, for in Christ we have the victory over evil anyway. It is wise for a pastor to find his place of solitude away from the daily battleground.

The first fifteen minutes of solitary communion with the Lord are the hardest because it takes longer than that to quiet your spirit and rest in God. Most preachers stop praying alone too soon. If you need help, read your Bible devotionally, not for study or sermon preparation. Read the Word, and let its inspired phrases speak to your heart. You may need to take notes as the Lord speaks to you.

And then pray! We preachers are usually on display, and much of our praise is directed more at encouraging others than for our own worship. In the loudest of "Bless God!" preachers there is a little child's voice that wants to cry out, "Abba, Father!" Preacher, your real spirituality will come to light when no one is watching. Set your pride and your public image aside and come weeping before Him as a little child. Jesus said, "Verily I say unto you, Whosoever shall not receive the kingdom of God as a little child shall in no wise enter therein" (Luke 18:17).

If we were in your church, we would start a little organ music about now. Don't be embarrassed. Don't be ashamed. Let your Heavenly Father take you in His arms. Forget your problems, your cares, the woes of pastoring. "The eternal God is thy refuge, and underneath are the everlasting arms: and he shall thrust out the enemy from before thee; and shall say, Destroy them" (Deuteronomy 33:27).

> It's me, it's me, oh Lord,
> Standing in the need of prayer.
> It's me, it's me, oh Lord,
> Standing in the need of prayer.

Speak in other tongues. Out loud! Shout the praises of the Lord God! Make up your heart and mind that if nobody else in the world is revived, you will be. Peter said, "Feed the flock of God which is among you, taking the oversight thereof, not by constraint, but willingly; not for filthy lucre, but of a ready mind" (1 Peter 5:2). Don't pastor that flock just because you have to but because you want to. Don't do it just for money but out of a driving vision of what God wants you to do. The word "ready" is a poor translation of *próthumos*, which means "eager in spirit" or "charging forward with a desire." When you come out of your solitude, return to your task like Moses coming down from Mount Sinai, with your face aglow and the Word of God in your hands!

Once you are revived in your spirit, there are seven things you must do to have a Pentecostal revival in your church.

1. *Pray.* There is no easy road to revival, no route but the way of the cross. It may be humiliating or painful, but the only path that leads to experience with God is through the Lord Jesus Christ. He is "the way, the truth, and the life," and no one comes to the Father but by Him (John 14:6). Only through prayer may you guide your people through the necessary steps of remorse, repentance, and revival. Nationally, the Assemblies of God announced a sacred assembly to call the whole Fellowship to repentance with prayer and fasting. Do something similar in your church—call a day of repentance to turn your church around and head it in the right direction for revival.

Make your prayer meeting a prayer meeting! Use your midweek service to prepare the church spiritually for Sunday. Small-group Bible studies and fellowship groups are an important part of most growing churches, but there also are times when the whole body needs to come together for prayer.

2. *Revive your Sunday night services!* You won't have any trouble gathering a crowd if the word gets out that the sick are being healed, people bound by the sins and substances of the world are being delivered, and all kinds of miracles are taking place. Be Pentecostal! If Jesus thought He needed signs and wonders to accomplish His work, how do you think you will carry out your task with anything less?

You need an atmosphere of worship in your services, but do not allow the music and praise to overshadow the preaching of the Word. Save some of the people's response for after the sermon.

3. *Preach the Word under a strong anointing.* Die to your old self and let the light of Christ shine through you to the congregation. Preach every sermon as though it were your last impassioned appeal for the cause of Christ. According to an old Scottish folk tale, when King Robert the Bruce of Scotland died, his people kept his heart in a special container, or casket. In a great battle with the English, the Scots carried the container to war with them as an encouragement to their troops. As they were being driven back toward defeat, someone grasped the casket and flung it far into the enemy lines, shouting, "There goes the heart of Bruce!" And the Scots surged forward to victory. Pastor, put your heart into the battle. Fling it into the fray and fight for revival like you're never coming back!

4. *Give altar calls!* If God inspires your preaching, He also intends that you give the people an opportunity to respond. Invite sinners to repent at the altar, but also call forward the whole congregation to seek the face of God. Paul wrote, "Quench not the Spirit" (1 Thessalonians 5:19). Allow the people to respond to God even if they become emotional, for it is in that setting of spiritual awareness and expectancy that they are saved, baptized in the Holy Spirit, healed, delivered, and motivated to holiness. Pray for the needs of the people, anoint the sick with oil, and when necessary cast out devils. Don't leave such leadership to anyone else; the anointing is on the preacher,

155

so you lead the altar ministries. The Lord is there, so expect something spiritual to happen in every service.

5. *Allow the gifts of the Spirit to operate in the services.* Remember that "the manifestation of the Spirit is given to every man to profit withal" (1 Corinthians 12:7). That is, the Spirit operates through individuals for the benefit of the whole body of believers. First Corinthians 14:4 says that speaking in tongues (without an interpretation) builds up the individual, but the manifestation of the gift of prophecy builds up the whole church. These and other verses indicate that we are supposed to have the operation of the gifts in the services.

6. *Once the revival has begun, set new short-term and long-range goals for your church.* In a revived church many things will change, so reevaluate everything and plan to maintain the revival flow. Not every service will be enthusiastic and joyful. Sometimes there will be a spirit of weeping over the sins of humanity, and at other times there may be laughter. The pastor must remain in close communication with the Lord so that he knows what to preach and how to conduct the service.

7. *Get people saved.* If your revival is not getting souls saved, it is going awry! Go back to your place of solitary prayer and ask God how to turn the course of your revival toward soul winning. It may take a while, because not all the results are immediate; nevertheless, the preaching of the Cross and the salvation of the lost must be uppermost on your agenda. You will find that from a revived church many young people will respond to the call of God and enter the ministry, thus multiplying manifold your own personal evangelistic efforts.

People are saying there is revival in the air. If they mean there is an air of expectancy today, then it is true. But revival is not an atmosphere, it is a relationship with the Lord Jesus Christ through the Holy Spirit.

When Peter was in prison and chained between two guards, a group of concerned Christians gathered to pray for him at the home of Mary the mother of John Mark. No doubt it was a powerful prayer meeting as they interceded with God for Peter's deliverance.

At that very moment, the angel of the Lord came right through the prison bars and barriers and woke up Peter. The chains fells off, and the angel led him out of the prison as the iron gates opened of their own accord. Left standing free in the street, Peter went to the home where the Christians were still praying. The Lord had already answered their prayers, and they didn't know it!

When Peter knocked at the door of the gate, a young woman named Rhoda responded and, upon recognizing his voice, got so excited she ran to tell the others without letting him in! Peter could miraculously walk through the gates of the prison, but he couldn't get past the doors of the "church"!

Rhoda told the Christians that their prayers were answered, but they said she was mad. When she insisted it was Peter at the gate, they got into more discussion and decided she had seen his spirit as in a vision. They had prayed effectively, but they didn't know how to accept the Lord's miraculous answer when it came.

When at last they opened the door and saw Peter standing there, they were beside themselves with joy. Even then, they were so astonished that nobody invited him in. They finally let Peter into the house, and he told them how the angel of the Lord had delivered him from prison (Acts 12:3–17).

Our churches all over America are having wonderful services with sincere praise and worship, but most of our church life is happening behind closed doors with little expectation of any supernatural response to our prayers. Here we are praying for revival . . . and God has already answered! The revival has already begun! We must open our hearts to God and our churches to a lost and dying world!

Rhoda, open that door!

Endnotes

PAGE

17   "Prayer is an essential . . ." Charles G. Finney, *Revivals of Religion*, The Christian Classics, 700 Club Edition (Virginia Beach, Va.: CBN University Press, 1978), 45.

44   "One of the things . . ." Donald Gee, *After Pentecost* (Springfield, Mo.: Gospel Publishing House, 1945).

47   "From the beginning . . ." Charles T. Crabtree, *The Pentecostal Priority* (Springfield, Mo.: Gospel Publishing House, National Decade of Harvest, 1993), 8.

47   "For a number of years . . ." General Council Minutes, April 1914, 2.

48   "The prophet Joel . . ." George O. Wood to David A. Womack, 30 December 1993.

48   In the second General Council . . . General Council Minutes, 23 November 1914, 12.

55   "I can give a prescription . . ." "Dr. R. A. Torrey's Prescription," Walter B. Knight, *Knight's Master Book of New Illustrations* (Grand Rapids, Mich.: Wm. B. Eerdmans Publishing Company, 1956), 568.

57   "I promise not to . . ." Thomas E. Trask, transcript of his speech at the ceremony for his installation as general super-intendent, Assemblies of God Headquarters, Springfield, Missouri, 18 November 1993.

65   "The Assemblies of God . . ." James K. Bridges, "What Revival Means," *Pentecostal Evangel,* 11 February 1990, 22.

67   The Day of Pentecost . . . David A. Womack, "What Is the Meaning of Pentecost?" *Pentecostal Evangel,* 7 June 1992, 4.

71   "One of the great statements . . ." Glen D. Cole to David A. Womack, 11 January 1994.

89   "What is revival? . . . " Armon Newburn, "A Call to Revival," in *Like a Prairie Fire,* ed. Bob Burke (Oklahoma City, Okla.: Oklahoma District Council of the Assemblies of God, 1994).

89   In his book . . . Colin C. Whittaker, *Great Revivals* (Springfield, Mo.: Gospel Publishing House, 1986), 15.

91   "The root idea . . ." *Baker's Dictionary of Theology,* ed. Everett F. Harrison (Grand Rapids, Mich.: Baker Book House, 1960), s.v. "Holiness, Holy," by Paul S. Rees.

96   David Broughton Knox said . . . *Baker's Dictionary of Theology,* s.v. "Right, Righteousness," by David Broughton Knox.

100   "I am a little concerned . . ." David A. Womack, ed., *Pentecostal Experience: The Writings of Donald Gee* (Springfield, Mo.: Gospel Publishing House, 1993), 54.

109   "I have been concerned . . ." James K. Bridges to David A. Womack, 14 January 1994.

118   "Where churches are failing . . ." Glen D. Cole to David A. Womack, 11 January 1994.

119   "I am not so afraid . . ." Dwight L. Moody, "Revivals" (sermon delivered on Wednesday morning, August 2, 1899, at East Northfield, Mass.), in *Moody's Latest Sermons* (Chicago: The Moody Institute Colportage Association, 1906), 111.

120   "There is no excitement . . ." Ibid., 112.

141   "When a girl . . ." *Academic American Encyclopedia* (Grolier Electronic Publishing, Inc., 1993, Prodigy Interactive Personal Services), s.v. "Helen Rowland."

142   "What is needed . . . " Donald G. Bloesch, *The Crisis of Piety* (Grand Rapids, Mich.: William B. Eerdmans Publishing Company, 1968), 15.

143   "Whereas there . . . " Thomas E. Trask, General Presbytery Resolution titled "Holy Convocation," August 1991.

143   "Looking back . . . " George O. Wood to David A. Womack, 30 December 1993.

144   "Newspapermen went . . . " Knight, *Knight's Master Book,* 568.

147   "When the providence . . . " Finney, *Revivals of Religion,* 21–31.

147   "The world still . . . " Knight, *Knight's Master Book,* 567.